CONVERSATIONS
WITH SCRIPTURE:
THE LAW

CONVERSATIONS
WITH SCRIPTURE:

THE LAW

KEVIN A. WILSON

MOREHOUSE PUBLISHING
HARRISBURG / PENNSYLVANIA

Morehouse Publishing and the Anglican Association of Biblical Scholars thank the Louisville Institute for their interest in and support of this series.

Morehouse Publishing, P.O. Box 1321, Harrisburg, PA 17105

Morehouse Publishing, 445 Fifth Avenue, New York, NY 10016

Morehouse Publishing is an imprint of Church Publishing Incorporated.

Cover art courtesy of Réunion des Musées Natiouaux / Art Resource, New York. Chagall, Marc (1887–1985) © ARS, NY. "Moses Receives the Tablets of the Law," MBMC 388. Photo: Gerard Blot. Photo credit: Réunion des Musées Nationaux / Art Resource, New York. Musee National message biblique Marc Chagall, Nice, France.

Series cover design by Corey Kent

Series design by Beth Oberholtzer

Library of Congress Cataloging-in-Publication Data

A catalog record of this book is available from the Library of Congress.

Printed in the United States of America

06 07 08 09   10 9 8 7 6 5 4 3 2 1

Dedicated to the participants in all of the parish Bible studies
I have been honored to lead, especially those of
All Saints' Episcopal Church, Sunderland, Maryland;
Church of the Redeemer, Baltimore, Maryland; and
First Congregational Church, West Haven, Connecticut.

Almighty God, our eternal teacher, you have given the law to your people through your servant Moses, so that those who follow it might live in your presence: Grant that we who have been grafted into the tree of Israel may understand your law and by your commandments be drawn ever closer to you: through the one who fulfilled the law, Jesus Christ our Lord, who lives and reigns with you and the Holy Spirit, one God, now and forever.

"Surely, this commandment that I am commanding you today is not too hard for you, nor is it too far away. It is not in heaven, that you should say, 'Who will go up to heaven for us, and get it for us so that we may hear it and observe it?' Neither is it beyond the sea, that you should say, 'Who will cross to the other side of the sea for us, and get it for us so that we may hear it and observe it?' No, the word is very near to you; it is in your mouth and in your heart for you to observe." (Deut 30:11–14)

> "Oh, how I love your law!
>   It is my meditation all day long.
> Your commandment makes me wiser than my enemies,
>   for it is always with me.
> I have more understanding than all my teachers,
>   for your decrees are my meditation."
>   (Psalm 119:97–99)

CONTENTS

INTRODUCTION
TO THE SERIES

To talk about a distinctively Anglican approach to Scripture is a daunting task. Within any one part of the larger church that we call the Anglican Communion there is, on historical grounds alone, an enormous variety. But as the global character of the church becomes apparent in ever-newer ways, the task of accounting for that variety, while naming the characteristics of a distinctive approach becomes increasingly difficult.

In addition, the examination of Scripture is not confined to formal studies of the kind addressed in this series of parish studies written by formally trained biblical scholars. Systematic theologian David Ford, who participated in the Lambeth Conference of 1998, rightly noted that although "most of us have studied the Bible over many years" and "are aware of various academic approaches to it," we have "also lived in it" and "inhabited it, through worship, preaching, teaching and meditation." As such, Ford observes, "The Bible in the Church is like a city we have lived in for a long time." We may not be able to account for the history of every building or the architecture on every street, but we know our way around and it is a source of life to each of us.[1]

That said, we have not done as much as we should in acquainting the inhabitants of that famed city with the architecture that lies within. So, as risky as it may seem, it is important to set out an introduction to the highlights of that city—which this series proposes to explore at length. Perhaps the best way in which to broach that task is to provide a handful of descriptors.

The first of those descriptors that leaps to mind is familiar, basic, and forever debated: *authoritative*. Years ago I was asked by a colleague who belonged to the Evangelical Free Church why someone with as much obvious interest in the Bible would be an Episcopal priest. I responded, "Because we read the whole of Scripture and not just the parts of it that suit us." Scripture has been and continues to play a singular role in the life of the Anglican Communion, but it has rarely been used in the sharply prescriptive fashion that has characterized some traditions.

Some have characterized this approach as an attempt to navigate a *via media* between overbearing control and an absence of accountability. But I think it is far more helpful to describe the tensions not as a matter of steering a course between two different and competing priorities, but as the complex dance necessary to live under a very different, but typically Anglican notion of authority itself. Authority, you see, shares the same root as the word "to author" and as such, refers first and foremost, not to the *power* to *control* with all that both of those words suggest, but to the capacity to *author creativity*, with all that both of those words suggest.[2] As such, the function of Scripture is to carve out a creative space in which the work of the Holy Spirit can yield the very kind of fruit associated with its work in the Church. The difficulty, of course, is that for that space to be creative, it is also necessary for it to have boundaries, much like the boundaries we establish for other kinds of genuinely creative freedom—the practice of scales for concert pianists, the discipline of work at the bar that frees the ballerina, or the guidance that parents provide for their children. Defined in this way, it is possible to see the boundaries around that creative space as barriers to be eliminated, or as walls that provide protection, but they are neither.

And so the struggle continues with the authority of Scripture. From time to time in the Anglican Communion, it has been and will be treated as the raw material of buttresses that protect us from the complexity of navigating without error the world in which we live. At other times, it will be treated as the ancient remains of a city to be cleared away in favor of a brave new world. But both approaches are rooted, not in the limitations of Scripture, but in our failure to welcome the creative space we have been given.

For that reason, at their best, Anglican approaches to Scripture are also *illuminative*. William Sloan Coffin once observed that the problem with Americans and the Bible is that we read it like a drunk uses a lamppost. We lean on it, we don't use it for illumination.[3] Leaning on Scripture—or having the lamppost taken out completely—are simply two very closely related ways of failing to acknowledge the creative space provided by Scripture. But once the creative space is recognized for what it is, then the importance of reading Scripture illuminatively becomes apparent. Application of the insight Scripture provides into who we are and what we might become is not something that can be prescribed or mapped out in detail. It is only a conversation with Scripture, marked by humility that can begin to spell out the particulars. Reading Scripture is, then, in the Anglican tradition a delicate and demanding task, that involves both the careful listening for the voice of God and courageous conversation with the world around us.

It is, for that reason, an approach that is also marked by *critical engagement* with the text itself. It is no accident that from 1860 to 1900 the three best-known names in the world of biblical scholarship were Anglican priests, two of whom were Bishops: B. F. Westcott, J. B. Lightfoot, and F. J. A. Hort. Together the three made contributions to both the church and the critical study of the biblical text that became a defining characteristic of Anglican life.

Of the three, Westcott's contribution, perhaps, best captures the balance. Not only did his work contribute to a critical text of the Greek Testament that would eventually serve as the basis for the English Revised Version, but as Bishop of Durham he also convened a conference of Christians to discuss the arms race in Europe, founded the Christian Social Union, and mediated the Durham coal strike of 1892.

The English roots of the tradition are not the only, or even the defining characteristic of Anglican approaches to Scripture. The church, no less than the rest of the world, has been forever changed by the process of globalization, which has yielded a rich *diversity* that complements the traditions once identified with the church.

Scripture in Uganda, for example, has been read with an emphasis on private, allegorical, and revivalist applications. The result has

been a tradition in large parts of East Africa which stresses the reading of Scripture on one's own; the direct application made to the
contemporary situation without reference to the setting of the original text; and the combination of personal testimony with the power
of public exhortation.

At the same time, however, globalization has brought that tradition into conversation with people from other parts of the Anglican
Communion as the church in Uganda has sought to bring the biblical text to bear on its efforts to address the issues of justice, poverty,
war, disease, food shortage, and education. In such a dynamic envi-
ronment, the only thing that one can say with certainty is that neither the Anglican Communion, nor the churches of East Africa, will
ever be the same again.

Authoritative, illuminative, critical, and varied—these are not the
labels that one uses to carve out an approach to Scripture that can be
predicted with any kind of certainty. Indeed, if the word *dynamic*—
just used—is added to the list, perhaps all that one can predict is still
more change! And, for that reason, there will be observers who (not
without reason) will argue that the single common denominator in
this series is that each of the authors also happens to be an Anglican.
(There might even be a few who will dispute that!)

But such is the nature of life in any city, including one shaped by
the Bible. We influence the shape of its life, but we are also shaped
and nurtured by it. And if that city is of God's making, then to force
our own design on the streets and buildings around us is to disre-
gard the design that the chief architect has in mind.

—Frederick W. Schmidt
Series Editor

AUTOBIOGRAPHICAL NOTE

It was in college that I made the decision to become a biblical scholar. I had entered my undergraduate studies as a religion major, planning to become a pastor. In my second year, however, something happened that changed that. I wanted to take a biblical language to increase my understanding of the Bible. The college I attended had enough interested students to offer Greek every year, but only enough interest for a Hebrew class every other year. By chance—or divine providence— Hebrew was offered my second year. Since everyone took Greek, I decided to take Hebrew. I immediately fell in love with the language. For one thing, Hebrew is written right-to-left, and as a left-handed person this was the first language that I didn't smear across the page as I wrote. But I was also drawn to the beauty of the language and the entirely new world I discovered in the pages of the Old Testament.

Since that time, I have constantly found myself attracted to the 'odd' parts of the Bible. These are the parts that almost no one reads, the parts that make people wonder why God would include these books in the Bible. If there is a section of the Bible where people question how we can hear God through these texts, I instantly want to discover how God *does* speak to us in these texts. I am convinced that God communicates with the church in all of the Bible, but I will admit that some sections require us to listen more closely than others.

The law of the Old Testament certainly falls into this category. In the church, we tend to regard the legal sections of the Pentateuch as important for ancient Israel but irrelevant for modern life. Although we enjoy the stories of Adam, Abraham, Moses, and the other characters in the Torah, many people not only do not understand the law but see no reason to take the time to try. Because of this, I have been drawn to the study of the legal material and the way it can be understood as the word of God for us today.

The fact that you have picked up this book suggests that you are interested in that question as well. My prayer is that the chapters that follow will help you explore the issue. May God use this book to open to you an exciting new area of the Bible.

Kevin A. Wilson
Klaipeda, Lithuania
March 25, 2006

INTRODUCTION

The first five books of the Bible, commonly known as the Pentateuch or Torah, contain many of the best-known stories in the Bible. From the creation stories and Noah's ark to the story of Israel's deliverance from Egypt under Moses, these tales have been read repeatedly within the church and are part of the common stock of stories that make up the biblical knowledge of most Christians. With the exception of Genesis, however, most of the Torah is composed not of stories but of laws. And while the stories are well-known, most of the legal sections are hardly ever read by Christians. Except for the Ten Commandments, Christians simply don't pay much attention to the laws of the Pentateuch.

Pentateuch/Torah: the first five books of the Old Testament: Genesis, Exodus, Leviticus, Numbers, and Deuteronomy. The term *Pentateuch* comes from a Greek term meaning "the five scrolls."

The Law in the Church and Israel

Part of the reason for the neglect of the law within Christianity stems from our historical position on this side of the New Testament. It is often assumed that because we now have Christ, we no longer need the law. For most Christians, their first encounter with the law comes through the writings of the New Testament, particularly those of the Apostle Paul. In his epistles, or letters, especially the Letter to the Romans and the Letter to the Galatians, Paul takes great pains to contrast the law with grace. Law, he asserts, does not bring salvation; only faith in Christ Jesus does (Gal 2:16). And Peter, in his speech to the council in Jerusalem, asks why the Jewish believers want Gentile believers to follow the

law. Why, he says, would you place on the Gentiles "a yoke that neither our ancestors nor we have been able to bear?" (Acts 15:10).
Because of this, many Christians have seen the law as opposed to
grace. If we live our lives by faith and are saved by grace, there is little
place for the law.

But that understanding of the law is quite different from the one
in the Old Testament. Rather than a burden that they were unable to
bear, the Israelites saw the law as a gift from God. They rejoiced that
they followed a God as wonderful as Yahweh, who gave them the
divine law:

> "For what other great nation has a god so near to it as the LORD our
> God is whenever we call to him? And what other great nation has
> statutes and ordinances as just as this entire law that I [Moses] am set-
> ting before you today?" (Deut 4:7–8)

Following this law brought about the greatest joy, causing the
psalmist to say, "I delight to do your will, O my God; your law is
within my heart" (Ps 40:8). The law was a means of life for the people of ancient Israel. God, who loved them, had given them this law
so they might receive the blessings that came from following it.

If you need to be convinced of the place of the law in ancient
Israel, just read Psalm 119. This chapter—perhaps not coinciden-
tally the longest in the Bible—is an extended song of praise of the
law. Set up as an acrostic, with each set of eight verses beginning
with the same letter of the Hebrew alphabet, the poem describes
those who keep God's commandments. They are called happy (vv.
1–2); the law is their delight (vv. 14–16); they experience freedom (v.
45); and they have comfort from God (v. 50). Almost every single
verse contains one of eight synonyms for the law, explaining how the
law benefits those who follow it. The psalmist hardly thought God's
statutes to be a burden but instead expressed his love for the law (v.
97). The prominent place it had in the life of the people is reflected
not only in the text but in the shape of the Old Testament canon as
well. The Pentateuch begins the story of the people of Israel.

If this was the view of the law in the Old Testament, then maybe
we Christians should rethink our approach to it. After all, Jesus himself affirmed its importance when he said he had come not to abol-

ish the law but to fulfill it (Matt 5:17–20) and that those who do and teach the commandments will be called great in the kingdom of heaven. Just as the Gospels are central to the story of who we are as Christians, the Pentateuch—both the narratives and the law—is central to the identity of Israel. If we as Christians take the Old Testament seriously as Christian Scripture, we need to pay attention to the law, allowing it to shape our theological and spiritual identity as the people of God.

Torah: although often translated "law," *torah* more accurately refers to instruction or teaching.

Definition of the Law

The word "law" as used in the Bible and in this book is a translation of the Hebrew word *torah*. The word has come to be translated "law" in English because the Septuagint, the Greek version of the Old Testament, used the Greek word *nomos* as the equivalent of *torah*. But while "law" is a faithful rendering of *nomos*, it is not the best translation of *torah*. "Law" implies a connection with an official set of rules by which the courts try cases. But the nature of the law in the Old Testament is something very different. A better translation—more faithful to the Hebrew as well as to the character of the law in the Pentateuch—is the word "instruction." The *torah* is God's instructions to the people of Israel. Just as a human teacher can instruct students (Ps 78:1; Prov 1:8), so can God instruct Israel. God's law informs them how they are to live as the people of God, a people God established through the exodus from Egypt. The law in the Bible sets out the principles by which the people of God were to order their lives, both as individuals and as a community.

Septuagint: the Greek translation of the Old Testament. It is called the "Septuagint" because of the tradition that it was produced by 70 translators in 70 days. It is abbreviated LXX, the Roman numeral for 70.

Let's look at Psalm 119 again to get an idea of the scope and breadth of the concept conveyed by the term *torah*. This psalm contains eight different synonyms for the *torah*: law, word, precept, ordinance, statute, commandment, decree, and way. Although these words are used in other parts of the Hebrew Bible in ways that are meant to denote specific types of laws, in Psalm 119 they further define what God's instruction is. Taken together, they indicate the

Exodus: God's delivery of the people of Israel from slavery in Egypt.

whole of God's guidance of the people and the various ways God teaches the people. The last of the synonyms, "way," is perhaps the best expression of God's *torah*. To follow the *torah* is to walk in the way of God.

Psalm 119 doesn't just talk about the *torah* as given at Mount Sinai and written down in the first five books of the Bible. Instead, it refers to any of God's instructions, regardless of how they come. Abraham was said to keep God's instructions (Gen 26:5) even though he lived centuries before God gave the law to Moses. And Moses was not the only one who delivered God's instruction. The law could be taught by God (Ps 94:12). It could be passed down from ancestors (Ps 78:5). Or it could be placed within the hearts of the people (Pss 37:31; 40:8). Only later, when God's instructions were written down and collected, did *torah* become synonymous with the written law in the Pentateuch.

Now that you've explored this broader understanding of the nature of Old Testament law, you might wonder why the title of this book is still *Conversations with Scripture: The Law*. If "instruction" or "way," for instance, is a better translation of the word *torah*, why not change the title of the book? The answer is a practical one. The translation of *torah* as "law" is so embedded in both scholarly and popular discussion of the Pentateuch that to change it would only bring about confusion. "Law" has become a technical term that covers the non-narrative sections of the Pentateuch, and for better or worse it will remain that way. For that reason, I've retained the traditional translation. But I hope that you, as you read this book, will keep the broader definition of the word *torah* in mind.

Development of the Law

In its earliest stages, the law was not written down. As in all ancient societies, few people in Israel could read or write, and manuscripts were difficult to produce by hand. In the time of the ancient Israelites, the best way to spread—and preserve—the law was to pass it on orally from teacher to student, from parents to children, from priests and prophets to people. When the psalmist says that the law is in the hearts of the people (Pss 37:31; 40:8), this is more than

> The law of their God is in their hearts; their steps do not slip. —Ps 37:31

just poetic flourish. In an oral culture, the law had to be learned "by heart," or it would not be learned at all.

Covenant: an agreement between two parties that imposes obligations and rights upon both parties

As time went by, certain laws were considered to be so important that the Israelites began collecting them and writing them down, not to replace the oral teaching of the law but to reinforce it. And because these laws regulated the lives of the people within the covenant, it was natural that the giving of these laws became associated with the making of the covenant at Mount Sinai following their exodus from Egypt.

But this association is secondary to the exodus story: if the legal material from Exodus 19— through Numbers 10 is removed, the resulting narrative still flows smoothly. Moreover, some passages in the Old Testament that provide us with short summaries of the story of Israel also leave out the giving of the law (Deut 26:5–9; Josh 24:2–13). Both of these facts suggest that the law was not originally part of the exodus story.

But the placement of the giving of the law at Mount Sinai is important. It expresses the theological conviction that this law is fundamental to what it means to be the people of God. If the experience of the exodus from Egypt defined the beginnings of Israel's life with God, then the law defined what it meant to continue to live as the people of God.

Source criticism: the branch of biblical studies that seeks to determine the compositional layers to biblical books. Within the Pentateuch, four such layers have been determined: Yahwist (J), Elohist (E), Deuteronomy (D), and Priestly (P).

If the law codes seem to have been separate from the narrative originally, we need to ask how the Torah arrived at its final form. This task is known as source criticism. Source criticism seeks to outline how originally oral traditions come to be collected and written down in the form that we have now. Although we'll look more closely at individual layers of material within the Pentateuch in the following chapters, let's start by exploring the basics.

Two major groups of legal material make up the Torah. The first of these, known as the priestly material, is designated by the letter P. The P source was written down during the sixth century BCE

P source: A source of the Pentateuch that originated in priestly circles when the people of Judah were living in exile in the Babylonia. The Babylonian Empire, which had its center in what would be modern Iraq, had destroyed the city of Jerusalem and its temple in 587 BCE. Many of the Israelites were deported to Babylon, where they had to find their way in the midst of a foreign culture. Fearful of losing their national and religious identity, the Israelites pulled together a number of narrative and legal texts and wove them together into their national story. As the name of the source suggests, scholars believe the priests were probably responsible for this work. Most of the legal material in Exodus, Leviticus, and Numbers comes from the P source, with additional narrative information supplied by two sources known as the Yahwist (J) and Elohist (E). Scholars think this form of the law may have circulated in the south of Israel, as it seems to have been the form used by the official priesthood in Jerusalem.

The second group of legal texts is found in Deuteronomy and is therefore referred to as the D source. This material in its written form dates from the late seventh century BCE and may have originated in the northern part of Israel. The D source seems to have been a minority opinion within ancient Israel, serving as a counter to the official law proclaimed by the priests in Jerusalem. Deuteronomy was probably added to the work of the priestly writer sometime around the end of the Babylonian exile in 538 BCE. When that occurred, the Torah reached its final stage of development, achieving the form in which we now have it.

The idea that four sources—JEDP—came together to form the Pentateuch is commonly called the documentary hypothesis. Although scholars often refer to these sources as if they were authors, remember that each "author" was probably a group of people pulling together material from a number of oral and written sources. In some passages, it is possible to isolate even earlier sources of the law, such as the Book of the Covenant (Exod 20:22–23:33), that JEDP have incorporated into their work. But while the material was written down in the seventh through fourth centuries before Christ, the traditions within the material often go back much further.

Outline of the Book

With the exception of chapter 1, the chapters in this book are arranged to follow the order of the laws in the Old Testament. Chapter 1 begins with the Ten Commandments, arguably the most important set of laws in the Pentateuch. The Bible actually contains two versions of the Ten Commandments—one in Exodus 20 and the other in Deuteronomy 6. After we explore the Commandments, we'll look at the law book by book through the Pentateuch. Chapter 2 deals with the laws in Exodus that follow the Ten Commandments, most importantly the Covenant Code in Exod 21–23. Chapters 3 and 4 look at the book of Leviticus, starting with the sacrificial law. Chapter 5 discusses the laws in Numbers, and the final chapter focuses on the laws in Deuteronomy, a law code very different from the laws in the rest of the Torah.

In each chapter we'll take a look at the laws in that section of the Torah and at the background in which they were set. Although different laws sometimes require a different approach, I'll try to explain the rationale behind the laws and the way they functioned in the life of ancient Israel. A final section in each chapter explores ways that the laws of the Pentateuch apply to the life of the church today. Throughout each of the chapters, I invite you to come to the law with an ear toward hearing God's word to the church today and an expectation that God continues to speak to us through these texts. I hope this book will serve as a call to a fresh understanding and appreciation of the law of God, a law that the people of Israel considered to be the greatest gift they could receive.

CHAPTER ONE

The Ten Commandments

The Ten Commandments are a part of our Judeo-Christian heritage. Some even go so far as to claim that our civil laws are derived from the Ten Commandments. Such a claim is questionable, however. A quick glance at the Decalogue demonstrates this. Out of the ten laws, only three are reflected in modern law: the prohibitions against murder, theft, and the bearing of false witness in court. The other seven are not a part of our laws. In place of the first commandment to worship only God, the United States and many other countries have laws that guarantee the right to worship any god or no god at all. These same laws also prohibit laws against idols. While blue laws used to prevent business from operating on Sunday, most places have taken these laws off the books, and there is now no connection between the civil law and the commandment to honor the Sabbath. Dishonoring one's father and mother isn't a crime, and while adultery may be grounds for divorce, it is not an arrestable offense in most places. And as for coveting, most advertising is geared toward getting us to covet the goods the advertisers are selling, and there is certainly no law against it.

The Centrality of the Ten Commandments

While the Ten Commandments have little to do with our secular law, it's impossible to overstate their centrality to our Christian moral systems. Most people who grow up in the church memorize these laws at one time or another, and even those who enter the church as adults are generally familiar with their content. Many churches even display the Ten Commandments in their sanctuaries and Sunday school classrooms. With the possible exception of some of the psalms and a few of the stories, the Ten Commandments are probably one of the most familiar parts of the Old Testament.

This centrality is not accidental. It's rooted in the Bible itself, where the Ten Commandments are accorded a special status among the laws of the Torah. This is clear from the two passages that preserve the Decalogue, Exod 20:1–17 and Deut 5:6–21.

In Exodus 20, God has delivered the people from Egypt through the exodus and they have journeyed to Mount Sinai, where Moses tells them to prepare themselves for God's appearance. During the theophany, God delivers the Ten Commandments directly to the people. Having heard God's voice, however, the people fear that they will die, and they ask Moses to act as an intermediary: "You speak to us, and we will listen; but do not let God speak to us, or we will die" (Exod 20:19). From that point on, God speaks the law to Moses, who relays it to the people. The direct delivery of the Ten Commandments, combined with their position as the first laws given to the people, highlights the centrality of these laws to the ancient Israelites.

> **Theophany:** an occasion when God is physically manifested to people, usually involving sight and/or sound

Deuteronomy also reinforces this impression through its placement of the Decalogue. Deuteronomy is set up as an address by Moses to the people of Israel as they prepare to enter Canaan. The book begins with a series of instructive sermons by Moses in chapters 1–11 that retell the events that have led the people to this point. Then the writer goes on to a second presentation of the law in chapters 12–26. But the Ten Commandments are not given as part of the law but placed at the beginning of the law as part of Moses' recitation of the history of the people. As in Exo-

> "You speak to us, and we will listen; but do not let God speak to us, or we will die." —Exod 20:19

dus, the Ten Commandments are once again delivered directly to the people, who then ask that Moses be the mediator for the rest of the law (Deut 5:22–26).

But when did the Ten Commandments become the centerpiece of the law? They had certainly obtained this status by the time of the writing of Deuteronomy and Exodus in the seventh and sixth centuries, respectively. But there are surprisingly few references to these laws as a set prior to that time. Hosea seems to refer to them in his criticism of the people, when he accuses them of lying, murdering, stealing, and committing adultery (Hos 4:2). Jeremiah likewise records a list similar to the Ten Commandments. In his Temple Sermon, Jeremiah chides the people: "Will you steal, murder, commit adultery, swear falsely, make offerings to Baal, and go after other gods that you have not known, and then come and stand before me in this house, which is called by my name, and say, "We are safe!"—only to go on doing all these abominations?" (Jer 7:9–10). While other passages in the prophets do refer to one or two of the Ten Commandments, these verses from Hosea and Jeremiah seem to be the only ones that regard the Decalogue as a set list of laws.

One possible explanation of why so few other passages refer to the Ten Commandments is that they didn't reach their final form until late in the monarchic period. Exodus was completed in the sixth century, while the section of Deuteronomy that contains the Decalogue is from only slightly earlier. In the centuries prior to this, the contents of the Ten Commandments may have been in flux. This is suggested by several passages in the Old Testament that preserve lists of laws that are similar to, but not identical to, the Ten Commandments. In fact, the Bible contains several Decalogue-like formulations, including those found in Exod 34:17–26; Lev 19:1–19; and Deut 27:15–26.

> **Monarchic period:** the period when Israel and Judah were ruled by kings. It began in the tenth century BCE with Saul and continued until the destruction of Jerusalem in 587 BCE.

The Top Ten List

To illustrate, let's take a look at two of these passages. Exod 34:17–26 contains a list of laws, only two of which are found in the Ten Commandments. Although the enumeration of these laws is unclear, it is possible to arrange them to form ten commandments:

1. Do not make cast idols.
2. Keep the Festival of Unleavened Bread.
3. Sacrifice all firstborn male animals to God.
4. No one shall appear before God empty-handed.
5. Keep the Sabbath.
6. Keep the Festival of Weeks, the Festival of Firstfruits, and the Festival of Ingathering.
7. Do not offer sacrifices with leaven.
8. Do not leave the sacrifice of Passover until the morning.
9. Bring the firstfruits of the ground to the temple.
10. Do not boil a kid in its mother's milk.

Of these, only the prohibition of idols and the keeping of the Sabbath are found in the Ten Commandments. The rest deal primarily with specific sacrifices and festivals. In this regard, it's interesting to note that within the Ten Commandments, the only festival law is the law concerning the Sabbath. Even the Passover, which is central to the salvation story of the Israelites, is left out of the Decalogue.

The laws of Lev 19:1–19, with a much longer catalogue, contain more laws that are parallel to the Ten Commandments. This list contains laws prohibiting stealing, swearing falsely, and bearing false witness. In addition, it includes a number of laws that cover topics ranging from unjust judgments and wage practices to the interbreeding of two different species of animals. There is only one law dealing with festivals, stipulating that the entire well-being offering must be eaten on the day it is offered. This passage also contains the commandment to "love your neighbor as yourself" (Lev 19:18), a law that Jesus called the second greatest commandment (Matt 22:39; Mark 12:31).

If these competing versions of laws were all circulating in the monarchic period, it's easy to see why the Ten Commandments were selected to serve as the center of Israelite law. Among the collections of laws surveyed here, the Decalogue is the one least tied to the land and to temple observances. Instead of expressing specific issues of how the Passover is to be observed, whether certain animals should be sacrificed, or how to keep the Feast of First-fruits, the Ten Commandments deal primarily with the overarching ideas concerning how the people are to relate to God and to others. In fact, the only law in the Ten Commandments that does deal with the observance of a specific day concerns the Sabbath. Originally, attendance at the temple or synagogue (a practice that began in the late postexilic period) wasn't required on the Sabbath—that day was merely a day of rest.

Postexilic period: the time after the people of Israel were allowed to return to Judah from their exile in Babylon. It began in 538 BCE when Cyrus, king of Persia, conquered Babylon and declared that all captive people may return to their homelands.

When Nebuchadnezzar in 597 BCE and 586 BCE took Israel into exile in Babylon, the "transportability" of the Ten Commandments was even more important. With the destruction of the temple, a number of religious festivals couldn't be observed at all, since Deuteronomy specified that such festivals could be observed only in Jerusalem (Deut 16:5–6). The Sabbath, however, could still be observed in Babylon, and it was in this period that it became the essential religious observance for Judaism.

Other laws of the Ten Commandments were also important in Babylon, as the people encountered the Mesopotamian gods. The call to worship Yahweh was even more urgent in this setting, and the remembrance that Yahweh was the God who had led them out of Egypt (Exod 20:2; Deut 5:6) inspired hope that God would once again remember the people and bring them out of their current captivity. The commandment against idols was also important in this period—it is reflected, for instance, in the message of Second Isaiah, who harangues those who fashion idols from wood: "No one considers, nor is there knowledge or discernment to say, 'Half of it I burned in the fire; I also baked bread on its coals, I roasted meat and have eaten. Now shall I make the rest of it an abomination? Shall I fall down before a block of wood?'" (Isa 44:19). Idolaters, he says, are too foolish to see that half of the wood is burnt to keep them warm, while the other half they consider to be a god.

Note that neither the Exodus 20 passage nor its parallel in Deuteronomy 5 refers to this set of laws as the Ten Commandments. In fact, the expression "Ten Commandments" isn't actually found in the Torah. The Hebrew phrase translated "Ten Commandments" literally means the "ten words." In Exodus, the only reference to the Ten Commandments comes in 34:28 and seems to refer to the laws in Exod 34:17–26. In Deuteronomy, Moses speaks of the Ten Commandments in 4:13, right before the recitation of the Ten Commandments. This reference, however, is a part of Moses' first speech in Deut 1:1–4:43, an introduction that was added to the book sometime after the second speech in chapters 12–28. In Deut 10:4, however, Moses does mention the Ten Commandments by name, making reference to the second set of tablets that God made after Moses broke the first set. Outside of these three occurrences, however, the phrase "the ten words" or "the ten commandments" occurs nowhere in the Old Testament. The fact that the references to the Ten Commandments are not directly associated with the Ten Commandments further strengthens the perception that these laws were not "set in stone" until late in the monarchic period.

Despite the fact that all Christian traditions hold the Ten Commandments to be a central statement, there is disagreement over the way we number them. Anglicans, as well as many others in the Reformed tradition, see the commandment to have no other gods as the first commandment, and the prohibition against idols as the second. Roman Catholics and Lutherans, however, combine these two into one commandment and divide the law against coveting into two commandments, one covering the neighbor's wife and the other covering all other possessions. The first division is suggested by the wording in Exodus, while the second follows that of Deuteronomy, but neither division affects the meaning of the commandments. In the discussion that follows, we'll use the Anglican division of the laws.

Our Relationship with God

The outline of the Ten Commandments falls neatly into two sections: the first four deal with our relationship with God, and the last six concern our relationships with others. Although only four laws address our behavior toward God, they are much longer than the last six laws. They also set the context for the interactions between people, as interpersonal relationships must be seen in the light of our relation to the divine.

The Ten Commandments open with the statement "I am the LORD your God." While not a commandment itself, it sets the context for the laws that follow. This phrase is found in other sections of the Pentateuch, most notably in the Holiness Code of Lev 17–26.[1] There, the complete phrase is "You shall be holy, for I the LORD your God am holy" (Lev 19:2). In Exodus and Deuteronomy, however, it refers not to the holiness of God but to the personal relationship between God and God's people. The word translated "LORD" here is the personal name of Yahweh, revealed to Moses at Mount Sinai (Exod 3:13–15).

Next comes a historical reminder: Yahweh is not some random god who has met the Israelites at Mount Sinai but the God who brought the people out of the land of Egypt and freed them from slavery. This is a crucial statement for understanding the Ten Commandments. These commandments are not moral absolutes given for all time. Instead, they are the stipulations of the covenant relationship made at Sinai between Yahweh and the people he has saved. These laws, as well as those that follow in the rest of Exodus, Leviticus, and Numbers, are to be understood as the requirements laid on the people by virtue of their willingness to enter into that covenant. The people are free to disobey the law, but if they do so, the covenant relationship with God is placed in danger.

After this introduction, the first commandment is given: "You shall have no other gods before me" (Exod 20:3; Deut 5:7). This commandment usually is understood to mandate monotheism among the people. And by the time of the closing of the biblical canon, this was probably the case. Within its earlier historical context, however, the existence of other gods was presupposed. This commandment, while not denying the reality of other gods, does prohibit worshiping them. Yahweh is not one god among many for the Israelites but rather the sole God of this people. God has redeemed this people for himself, and they are to worship him only. They may hold no other gods to be higher than or even equal to Yahweh.

The second commandment forbids the making of idols. In later tradition, people understood this as making a representation of Yahweh, the God of Israel. In Moses' first speech in Deuteronomy, he instructs the people, "Since you saw no form when the LORD spoke to you at Horeb out of the fire, take care and watch yourselves closely, so that you do not act corruptly by making an idol for yourselves, in the form of any figure" (Deut 4:15–16).

In the current wording of this law in the framework of the Ten Commandments, however, the law deals not with the worship of God but with the possibility that the people might make an idol in the form of anything, whether in heaven, on earth, or in the seas. As such, the law logically follows the first commandment. Not only are the people supposed to worship Yahweh alone; they are even forbidden from making idols of other gods or anything else that might be worshiped.

The law against idols continues with the statement that God is a jealous God who punishes children, grandchildren, and great-grandchildren for the sins of the parents. The idea that God is a jealous God is found in a number of places in the Old Testament (Exod 34:14; Deut 4:24; 6:15; Ezek 39:25; Joel 2:18; Zech 1:14; 8:2). It refers to God's unwillingness to share his people with other gods. They are to worship only Yahweh. This metaphor of jealousy is drawn from the realm of marriage. Yahweh wants an exclusive relationship with the people, just as the relationship between a husband and wife is exclusive.

The statement that God punishes the descendants for the sins of the parents may be a troubling statement for modern readers. We are not comfortable with the idea that an entire family could suffer for the sins of one. Moreover, this statement cannot be reduced to the idea that sin merely affects an entire family, because the verse states that it is God—and not merely the outworking of sin—who punishes these generations.

It is clear that even in ancient Israel some people found this concept problematic. During the early sixth century, when it was becoming clear that Babylon would soon destroy the kingdom of Judah, people had apparently taken up the saying, "The parents have eaten sour grapes, and the children's teeth are set on edge" (Jer 31:29; Ezek 18:2). They claimed that it was not *their* sins that were bringing on the destruction but the sins of their parents. Both Jeremiah and Ezekiel took up this proverb only to reject it, saying that the people were being punished for their own sins, not those of their ancestors.

Yet although the idea of corporate punishment for individual sins was certainly present in ancient Israel, the statement in the third commandment doesn't actually refer to the punishment of the children long after the parents have died. Instead, it refers to the punishment of all of the generations living together in an extended family—the punishment of an entire household for the sins of one member—not the passing on of a punishment to successive generations.[2] Much more important, but more often overlooked, is the statement that God shows mercy to the thousandth generation of those who love him and keep his commandments.

The third commandment forbids misusing the name "Yahweh," the personal name of God, revealed to Moses at Mount Sinai in his first encounter with God in Exod 3:13–16. Many modern English translations indicate the presence of the divine name of Yahweh in the original text by translating it as "LORD" and printing it in capital and small capital letters, distinguished from the standard Hebrew word for "Lord," rendered in capital and lowercase letters. Unfortunately, what it means to take the Lord's name in vain is far from clear. The idiom "to take up the name" occurs only in the Exodus and Deuteronomy versions of the Ten Commandments, so we have to infer the meaning of this phrase from just these two instances. Usually, it has been taken to indicate that God will punish those who believe his name carries no power. In the ancient Near East, the name of a person or a deity was considered to have a power of its own, and a blessing or curse pronounced in the name of the god would actually bring about the blessing or curse intended. For someone to hold that the name of God carried no power would be the same as stating that God was powerless. This command refers to a much more serious theological charge than merely using God's name as an expletive.

Interestingly, the Old Testament contains no account of anyone's misuse of the Lord's name. This makes the third commandment unique among the Ten Commandments. There are numerous examples of people who broke the other commands throughout the Hebrew Bible, with murder, adultery, and the worship of other gods topping the list, but no stories of anyone's wrongful use of God's name. The closest story is that of Lev 24:10–23, in which a man blasphemes the name of the Lord. But because it is unclear how closely blasphemy is related to the misuse of God's name, we can't assume the two are the same sin.

The fourth commandment covers the Sabbath. The name "Sabbath" is a transliteration of Hebrew, a noun form derived from the verb šbt, meaning "to cease, to stop." On the Sabbath, therefore, the people were required to cease all their labor, as well as that of their family, slaves, and animals. As the seventh day of the week, it ran from sundown on Friday night to sundown on Saturday night. By resting, the people set aside the Sabbath day as holy to the Lord.

The Sabbath law is also the only law that shows significant variation between the Exodus and Deuteronomy versions. While both begin with the same commandment to rest from labor, each gives a different rationale for the Sabbath. In Deuteronomy, the Israelites are told that they are to keep the Sabbath because God delivered them from slavery in Egypt, and so they should devote the day wholly to the Lord. In the same way that Christians worship on Sunday because it is the day of Jesus' resurrection, the Israelites were to keep the Sabbath as a remembrance of their salvation.

In Exodus, on the other hand, the Sabbath commandment is connected not with the creation of Israel as a people but with the creation of the world. In the story of creation in Genesis 1, the text reminds the people that God created the world in six days. In the same way, they are to labor for six days during the week and, just as God rested on the seventh day, to take a day of rest on the Sabbath. This grounding of the Sabbath in the creation story envisions a process through which people participate in the ongoing creation of the world. In ceasing their labor on the Sabbath, the Israelites participate in the renewal of creation—that is why not only humans are to rest but animals as well.

In other parts of the Old Testament law, the Sabbath regulation is expanded to include larger periods of time grouped at intervals of seven years. Exodus 23:10–11 requires the people to allow their land to remain uncultivated every seventh year. This resting of the land is not rooted in the agricultural practice of restoring the fertility of a field by allowing it to lie fallow. Instead, the law states that the reason for the sabbatical year is to provide for the poor and needy in the land, who were allowed to eat the produce that grew on its own during the seventh year. The same law occurs again in Lev 25:1–7, although in this passage the owners of the field are allowed to eat the produce as well.

In addition to the seven-year cycle of Sabbath years, a second cycle of seven times seven years was included as well. After the forty-nine-year cycle, a Jubilee Year was to be proclaimed in the fiftieth year. Leviticus 25:8–55 describes the various laws for this Jubilee, most of which have to do with land and houses being returned to their original owners. This practice prevented land from being sold in perpetuity so that property remained in the same family. It was also a means of preventing the cycle of poverty that can continue from one generation to the next. If the members of one generation, through bad luck, laziness, or any other reason, fell into poverty and were forced to sell their land, their children would still get the property back in the fiftieth year. This practice kept wealth from being concentrated in the hands of a few and allowed each generation to regain a means of making a living.

Our Relationships with Others

The focus on the entire family in the Sabbath regulation, as well as on foreigners who are living in Israel, serves as a hinge in moving between those laws that deal with our relationship with God and those that govern our interactions with others. The first in this category is the command to honor one's father and mother. Although some see this law as arising from the practice of ancestor worship in ancient Israel—after all, how can your living parents guarantee you long life?—in its current setting the fifth commandment deals with the relationship between the generations. At the time it was written, extended families were the norm, with three to four generations often living together in the same household. The commandment is aimed not so much at children, who were certainly expected to honor their parents, as at adults, who were expected to provide for their parents in old age. Jesus took the Pharisees to task for teaching people not to follow this verse because they taught that people could contribute to the temple the resources that should have been used to support their parents (Mark 7:9–13).

Precisely what the honoring of parents means is difficult to determine. The word *honor* has a very broad range of meaning. As biblical scholar Terence Fretheim succinctly puts it, "It is an open-ended commandment, inviting children to respond in any way that honors parents. In all dealings with parents, respect, esteem, having regard and concern for, and showing affection, considerateness, and appreciation are the order of the day."[3]

But it may be easier to define the word by looking at those actions that go against it, since it is usually easy to spot actions that break this commandment. Since few families live with more than parents and children in the same house today, the challenges in applying this commandment now include questions of extended health care for the elderly, nursing homes, and the dignity of life for those reaching the end of life.

The sixth commandment begins a series of negative commandments notable for their brevity: "You shall not murder. You shall not commit adultery. You shall not steal. You shall not bear false witness against your neighbor." Unlike the first five commandments, most of which contain expansions of the basic statement of the laws, these next four commandments contain no justification or explanation. Instead, they state the prohibited action and then move on, often using only two words in the Hebrew.

The sixth commandment prohibits murder, a fact that is reflected in modern translations. Older translations, such as the King James Version, obscure the specificity of the command by translating it as "Thou shalt not kill." This translation overlooks the distinction between different types of killing. While we may disagree with the Old Testament on issues of capital punishment and revenge, it is clear that these types of killing were not included under the prohibition of the sixth commandment. A number of Old Testament sins were punishable by the death penalty, although this form of punishment was often carried out by the community instead of being left to an official body such as the state. And although several laws curtail the extent and severity of revenge, avenging the murder of a family member was maintained as the duty of the closest male relative.

The seventh commandment, against adultery, prohibits sexual relationships by married people with anyone other than their spouse. Although faithfulness to the marriage relationship is certainly a part of this law, the primary reason for the command seems to have been the need to determine the paternity of children. Given the absence of genetic tests that could determine who the father was, the only way to ensure that a child was the offspring of the husband was to prohibit the husband and wife from having sex with others. Such paternity was important, since it determined not only who would inherit the property but also who would lead the family in the next generation. Men did not want to pass on property to a child who wasn't their own, and hence they needed a guaranteed way of knowing that their children were theirs.

Because of this, some scholars have suggested that the laws against adultery were aimed primarily at women. It's true that the most common use of the idea of adultery is by the prophets, who accused the people of committing adultery by going after others gods (Jer 3:6–10; Ezek 16:35–43; Hos 1–3). And in that metaphorical usage, Israel is identified as a woman who commits adultery. But within the laws of the Torah, including those of the Ten Commandments, the prohibition is always directed against men. In both Exod 20:14 and Deut 5:18, the negative command uses the second person masculine. If the intended addressee was primarily or exclusively women, the feminine form of the verb would have been used. The same use of the masculine is also found in Lev 20:10, the only other law in the Pentateuch that uses the verb for "adultery." There, it is the man who commits adultery with the wife of a neighbor, and both are considered to be guilty of adultery. It is clear that in ancient Israel adultery was not a sin limited to women.

Including men in the scheme of adultery expands their responsibility and also removes them somewhat from a position of power. Far from being free to roam sexually while their wives remain faithful, men must take responsibility as well. Instead of being focused on their own individual need to know the paternity of their children, they are to expand this concern to the society too. It is in the best interest of the people as a community to know the parentage of children, since not only inheritance but also matters of responsibility toward children depend on such knowledge. The men are to move beyond looking after the interests of their own family and, by refraining from adultery, help to ensure that other families are free from such problems as well.

"Do not steal" is the eighth commandment. Two verbs are used in the Old Testament that are commonly translated "to steal," *ganav* and *gazal*. The first is used in the Ten Commandments. While both involve the illegal possession of property that belongs to another, the difference between the two lies in the way the property came to be in the possession of the thief.[4] *Ganav* refers to property taken by illegal measures, the act that is prohibited here. *Gazal*, on the other hand, doesn't involve robbery. Instead, it refers to a situation in which the thief came into possession of the item lawfully but is unlawfully holding back the property from its owner. An example of this is found in Lev 19:13, where the verb *gazal* is paired with the act of holding back the wages of a laborer until morning. Although the employer came to have the wages in a lawful way—that is, they were his until the laborer earned them—the act of retaining them is taken to be stealing.

The ninth commandment prohibits bearing false witness against one's neighbor. While it is easy to imagine a general prohibition against lying, the original setting for this instruction is in a court of law. The practice of bearing false witness is, in fact, the practice of committing perjury in court by lying as part of your testimony. This can be seen from other examples of the idiom "to bear witness." In Num 35:30, for example, it is established that people may not be put to death when the evidence against them consists of the testimony of only one witness. Deut 19:15–20 describes a situation in which a false witness has come forward to make an accusation in court. So severe is this challenge to civil society that the punishment for such an act was that the perjurer, if found out, was to be given the same sentence that he sought to bring against his neighbor. In this way, the people of Israel would "purge the evil from [their] midst" (Deut 19:19).

The final commandment concerns coveting, the intense desire to own or possess something that belongs to someone else. Although it has been suggested that coveting involves the act of trying to obtain another person's property, that doesn't seem to be implicit in the meaning of the verb, which refers only to the impulse and desire to possess someone else's belongings. This is clear from passages such as Josh 7:21 and Mic 2:2, in which verbs such as *take* or *seize* must be used whenever the desire results in action. It can also be seen in the adjective form of this root, which means "desirable." This reference to desire sets the tenth commandment apart, as it is the only commandment that is concerned with inner disposition rather than outward action.

The wording differs between the Exodus and Deuteronomy versions of this commandment because of a change in order of things that are coveted. In Exodus, the prohibition is against coveting your neighbor's house, wife, slave, animals, or anything else. Deuteronomy covers basically the same objects but places "wife" at the head of the list instead of "house." This difference in wording is what prompts Roman Catholic and Lutheran commentators to split this verse into two commandments. As it stands, however, the commandment in Exodus is probably the earlier, with the house being understood as the household and everything in it. It was intended to be read as forbidding the coveting of the neighbor's household, namely, his wife, slaves, and so on. Deuteronomy moves the wife to the beginning of the list, not to suggest two commandments but to indicate that the wife is more important than the slaves or property belonging to the household.

Conversations with the Commandments

The Ten Commandments are used by churches everywhere, and it is difficult to overestimate their importance. But they also have their origins in a culture and time very different from our own; some issues we'd like to see discussed are simply not present. For example, when we read the law stating that children must honor their parents, we wonder how broadly we should understand that commandment, especially in instances in which the parent is abusive.

The problem of the limited nature of the Decalogue was in some ways already addressed by the other parts of the law in the Old Testament. Although the Ten Commandments are an important component of that law, they are only a small section of it. Any ethic that seeks to use the Ten Commandments, therefore, must recognize that they are part of a larger body of material and shouldn't be taken in isolation. They may summarize the law, but summaries are of only limited use. Specific instances also must be addressed, and in many ways the Ten Commandments provide no more than minimal guidance for wider application.

Within the Old Testament, we already see an attempt to expand on the Decalogue to cover other situations. The Sabbath commandment is a case in point. Whereas the Sabbath law covers only one day of the week, the Israelites took this understanding of the sanctification of an individual day and expanded it to apply to years as well, with the result being the Sabbatical and Jubilee years. The idea of a Sabbath rest gave them an internal rationale for the sanctification of larger periods of time. The expansion took into account not only the sanctification of time to God but also care for other human beings and the entire creation. On the Sabbath the people expressed this concern by allowing servants and animals to rest, while the Sabbatical Year required the owner of the land to give rest to the land and to allow the poor to eat the produce of the fields. The Jubilee Year required that all debts be forgiven and all land be returned to its original owner.

Such Old Testament expansions of the laws of the Decalogue provide us a precedent for engaging in the expansion of the law. To remain with the subject of the Sabbath, we can ask, for instance, how does both the sanctification of time and weekly rest inform our outlook on the work week? Do we understand our work to be so important that we can't take a day off to rest? If so, what does this say about our understanding of God's provision for us? Maybe it indicates that we believe it is our own work that provides us with the money for our daily needs—rather than God's gracious care. And as for the sanctification of time, what does it say about our relationship with God when we feel we can't afford to take one day out of our week to sanctify it to the Lord?

The fact that the Ten Commandments come from another time and culture also gives us a chance to enter into conversation with them about how they can inform our lives. For example, the commandment against coveting must be understood against a background very different from our own. In Old Testament times, if someone wanted something that someone else had, the only way to get it was to take it. If my neighbor had a cloak I wanted, then the only way to have that cloak was to deprive *him* of it—a very different situation than we know in the modern consumer market. Today if I want a cloak like my neighbor's, all I have to do is run down to the local store where there are twenty more just like it, providing I have the money to buy it. Coveting in the Old Testament led to depriving one's neighbor of his or her goods. Today coveting leads to a consumerism in which our every want is treated as a need and often can be fulfilled immediately. How does the tenth commandment criticize such a consumer culture, and what does it say about our desire to have more and more possessions?

The Commandments: Still Central after All These Years

The Ten Commandments hold a central place in the biblical record and the life of the church. They express the basic requirements of the life of faith within the community constituted by God. By reaching in both a vertical and a horizontal direction, they call us to the remembrance of the two most important commandments: love God, and love your neighbor. Despite the fact that these laws were written thousands of years ago, they are an elegant statement of what it means to live as the people of God. Although they don't provide a complete ethic, the biblical warrant is there for the expansion of the principles contained in these commandments to cover a variety of situations, including those not envisioned by the ancient Israelites. By entering into conversation with the Decalogue, we can allow it to critique our understanding of what it means to be in relationship with God and with other people.

CHAPTER TWO

The Law in Exodus

As important as the Ten Commandments are, they are not the only laws in the book of Exodus. God continues to give laws throughout the book of Exodus. The Book of the Covenant picks up where the Ten Commandments left off. The Israelites' relationship with God is then carried further in the giving of the laws describing the building of the tabernacle and the establishment of the priesthood.

> **Book of the Covenant/ Covenant Code:** an early law code that has been incorporated into Exod 20:22–23:33

We can look at these laws in Exodus in an abstract way, without reference to the surrounding material. To a certain extent, that is the purpose of this book, which focuses only on the law and not on the narrative sections of the Pentateuch. But the Bible doesn't present these laws as originating in a vacuum. They are always part and parcel of the narrative of Exodus.

Biblical scholar Terence Fretheim calls attention to the context of the law in his commentary on Exodus.[1] Each of the main sections of law, he says—the Ten Commandments (Exod 20:1–17), the Book of the Covenant (20:22–23:33), the instructions for the tabernacle and priesthood (25:1–31:18), and the building of the tabernacle (35:1–40:38)—is bracketed by narrative. The effect is to keep the law firmly rooted in the life of the people. And that is very important. Once law becomes removed from life and becomes a "law unto itself," it no longer works the way the biblical authors intended.

The most important narrative connected with the law is the exodus story in Exod 1–18. Woven into the cloth of the same big narrative, the law is not a divine directive imposed on the people from outside but part of the same plan as the deliverance from Egypt and the covenant at Sinai: God has called a people for his own. Delivering the people from Egypt, God saves them from their bondage. Giving them the law, God makes a covenant with them to be their God while they are God's people. The law flows from the people's salvation from Egypt, and if we read it apart from that salvation history, it becomes a dead legalism that can bring no life.

The Book of the Covenant

The laws that follow immediately after the Ten Commandments, in Exod 20:22–23:33, are known as the Book of the Covenant, or Covenant Code. The name of this section is taken from Exod 24:7, where Moses reads the Book of the Covenant to the Israelites, who accept the laws and agree to follow them. This section of the law is generally held to be the oldest of all the law codes found in the Bible.

Scholars disagree about the origins of the Book of the Covenant, although most concur that it wasn't originally part of the Sinai tradition. The content of the laws themselves, however, gives us many clues about the type of society in which they originated. Slavery was a part of the social order (Exod 21:2–11, 20–21, 26–27). The presence of laws governing problems with oxen (21:28–22:1) suggests that the laws come from a settled, agrarian society, since oxen are used primarily in the cultivation of fields. This is reinforced by the ordinances that cover instances in which fields have been overgrazed or accidentally set on fire (22:5–6), as well as stipulations that the firstfruits of the harvest must be given as an offering (22:29).

But this description could apply to Israel at any period in its history. A number of scholars have suggested that these laws come from the period before the rise of the monarchy in the tenth century BCE, since no mention is made of a king. This is hardly conclu-sive, though, as only Deuteronomy contains laws dealing with the king, and it is likely that even in the monarchic period the king played little role in administering local matters. In addition, Exod 23:19 mentions the "house of the LORD," which usually—but not always—refers to the temple, suggesting a period after Solomon built the temple in the second half of the tenth century BCE.

Regardless of their origin, however, it is clear that the laws in the Book of the Covenant went through several stages of editing. We can discern the earliest stage in the laws found in Exod 21:1–23:19. This section of the Book of the Covenant falls easily into two sections: 21:1–22:17 and 22:18–23:19. Scholars make this division because of the forms of the laws in the two sections. In the first section—which contains its own introduction in Exod 21:1—the laws are pri-marily in casuistic form, following a basic "If . . . then" format, often with expansions that cover variations on the initial law. Most of the laws also specify some sort of punishment. The second sec-tion, by contrast, contains mostly apodictic laws, which don't specify punishments but state simply "You shall . . . !" or "You shall not . . . !" At first, these two sections of laws were probably collected separately and circu-lated independently and only later were brought together to make up a single law code through a second stage of editing.

> **Casuistic law:** law that is aimed at particular circum-stances. It generally follows an "If . . . then . . ." pattern. "If someone is caught kid-napping another Israelite, enslaving or selling the Israelite, then that kidnapper shall die" (Deut 24:7) is an example of casuistic law.

A third stage of editing brought these two combined sections into the book of Exodus and placed them in their current setting. The editors also added a set of introductory laws (Exod 20:22–26) and a concluding exhortation (23:20–33) that differ greatly from the laws in the Book of the Covenant. The initial laws are concerned with religious matters such as the making of idols and the proper way to construct an altar. Aside from the law prescribing the death penalty for those who sacrifice to other gods (22:20), such concerns aren't present in the rest of the Book of the Covenant.

The concluding exhortation has even less in common with the Covenant Code. It contains no

> **Apodictic law:** laws that express universal commands or prohibitions. "You shall not murder" (Exod 20:13) is an example of apodictic law.

laws but instead instructs the Israelites to completely destroy the Canaanites after entering the Promised Land. These introductory and concluding sections provide a framework to the Book of the Covenant and help it fit into its place in the book of Exodus.

THEOLOGICAL SETTING OF THE COVENANT CODE

The location of the Book of the Covenant within Exodus is theologically significant. The Ten Commandments, of course, are the first laws given by God, so the placement of the Book of the Covenant right after the Ten Commandments shows how significant the Book of the Covenant actually is. The passages immediately following the Covenant Code also point to its importance, picking up the narrative that concludes what began in Exodus 19. In Exodus 24, the covenant is ratified through two ceremonies. In the first, Moses reads the Book of the Covenant to the people, who affirm that they will obey all that is written in it. Moses then makes several sacrifices that seal the covenant with God. In the second ceremony, God calls Moses, Aaron, and Nadab and Abihu (Aaron's oldest sons), along with seventy of the elders of Israel, to draw near to God. Once on the mountain, they are allowed to see God and enjoy a meal in God's presence.

The covenant-making process begun when the people arrived at Mount Sinai concludes with the sacrifices and the meal with the elders on the mountain. Between these two events, only two sets of laws have been given: the Ten Commandments and the Book of the Covenant. While more laws will be added to these in the rest of the book of Exodus as well as in Leviticus, Numbers, and Deuteronomy, the fact that these two laws are included within the covenant-making process itself point to the importance that they had in ancient Israel as well as the centrality biblical authors ascribe to them. If the writers of the Pentateuch had not considered the law important, they would not have connected it with the covenant at Sinai.

THE CONTENTS OF THE BOOK OF THE COVENANT

Although the Book of the Covenant is often referred to as the Covenant Code, this title isn't quite accurate. A "code" implies a fairly complete collection of laws that covers most situations—and that is beyond the scope of the Book of the Covenant. As a law code goes, it is a bit incomplete. While it contains laws about slavery, theft, injury, slander, and religious festivals, it leaves out most other areas of life. And most of the coverage is skimpy—for example, although Exod 22:5–6 gives laws concerning agricultural mishaps, including overgrazing and the burning of a field, many other situations aren't addressed at all. There are laws, for instance, that discuss the amount of restitution that must be paid when someone has stolen livestock (Exod 22:1) but none that cover other types of stolen goods. So it's best to think of the Book of the Covenant not as a complete law code but as a collection of rules never intended to be the sole law of the land.

The laws in the Book of the Covenant contain a number of parallels with other ancient Near Eastern law codes.[2] For example, Exod 21:2–6 is similar to a statute in the Laws of Ur-Nammu about male slaves marrying female slaves. In that code as in the Bible, the female slave isn't given her freedom if the male slave is freed (*RANE*, 105). Exodus 21:22–25 is paralleled by rules in the Laws of Lipit-Ishtar and the Code of Hammurabi (*RANE*, 107, 113–14), while Exod 21:35–36, a law concerning a goring ox, is found in the Laws of Lipit-Ishtar as well (*RANE*, 111). Exodus 21:28–32 also has parallels in the Laws of Lipit-Ishtar and Hammurabi (*RANE*, 111, 114).

These Mesopotamian law codes come from a number of periods. The Laws of Ur-Nammu are from around the twenty-first century BCE. The Laws of Lipit-Ishtar were written a century later, while the famous Code of Hammurabi dates to the eighteenth century BCE. Although these codes all predate the Book of the Covenant, it is unlikely that their similarity can be explained by direct borrowing of the laws, as some scholars have suggested. Instead, the Covenant Code, like the rest of the laws of the ancient Near East, probably forms a part of the same legal traditions common for millennia in Mesopotamia, Syria, and Palestine. Finding similar laws in different codes in the ancient Near East should be no more surprising than finding similar laws in the British and American legal system; both spring from a common tradition.

The two sections of the law (Exod 21:1–22:17 and 22:18–23:19) are not just expressed differently but also organized differently. The laws in the first section seem to have been ordered according to subject, while those in the second section seem to have been ordered randomly. For the most part, section 2 wanders from lending money to cursing to offerings to slander. Only at the end (23:10–19) does it group together laws concerning a similar subject (religious festivals), though even here the uniformity is broken by the prohibition against boiling a kid in its mother's milk, since scholars debate whether such boiling constitutes a ritual act or not.

The laws in the first section can be arranged in several different ways—the way I've divided them here isn't the only possibility. The first group comprises laws dealing with slaves (Exod 21:2–11). It begins with the stipulation that a male slave may serve for only six years and must be given his freedom in the seventh year. This law parallels that in Deut 15:12, which also limits slavery to six years. Female slaves apparently serve indefinitely, as Exod 21:7–11 suggests, although this may be because the master of the house is presumed to have taken her as a wife. The laws also provide for male slaves who decide that they prefer not to go free (Exod 21:5–6).

The second group of laws deals with personal injury (Exod 21:12–36; 22:2–3 may have originally belonged to this group), both intentional and unintentional, as well as injury caused by people, animals, and even pits dug in the ground. It is in this section that the well-known *lex talionis* is found. The *lex talionis*, Latin for "the law

Lex talionis: Latin for "the law of the claw." It refers to Exod 21:23–25, which requires life for life, eye for eye, tooth for tooth, etc.

of the claw," states, "You shall give life for life, eye for eye, tooth for tooth, hand for hand, foot for foot, burn for burn, wound for wound, stripe for stripe" (21:23–25). It is interesting to note that this law is not stated at the beginning of the section, as might be expected for a general principle, but is instead associated with a law covering injury to a pregnant woman (21:22). The reason for this placement is unclear. Unfortunately, the law is not applied universally in this section, as it doesn't apply to cases in which the slave is the victim, since the slave is considered the property of the owner (21:21).

The final group covers damage to property (Exod 22:1–17). These laws cover cases of theft, intentional and unintentional damage to cultivated fields, and disputes over ownership. In general, punishment for damage stipulates restitution of some type, with additional fines in certain cases. It may seem strange that laws concerning the seduction of a virgin are included in this section (22:16–17). Unfortunately, however, unmarried women were considered the property of their fathers. The loss of virginity meant that the father could not ask as high a price from a potential husband, and hence the punishment in this case is the payment of the bride-price. The woman may even be married to the offender if the father agrees; it doesn't appear that her wishes in the matter were considered important.

Bride-price: the amount of money paid by the groom to the bride's father in exchange for marrying the daughter.

The second section of laws (Exod 22:18–23:19) isn't organized by subject or according to any other discernable principle. The laws seem to be in an almost random order, although sometimes groups of two or three laws covering similar topics are placed together (for example, the three laws concerning court cases in 23:6–8). Any discussion of the laws in this section would therefore be rather disjointed, and as most of the laws are fairly easy to understand, a detailed treatment isn't necessary.

One notable set of laws, however, is the one dealing with the poor, the oppressed, and others who are economically disadvantaged. Although scattered throughout this second section, these laws exhibit a consistent concern for the poor and require God's people to take care of those without means. The justification for this is in Exod 22:21, where the people are reminded that they themselves were slaves in Egypt and therefore must show mercy to those who are in similar situations.

That mercy should manifest itself in very particular actions: the Israelites are not to charge interest on loans to the poor (Exod 22:25). If they take a neighbor's cloak in exchange for a loan, they are to return it each night to protect the poor from the elements (22:26–27). The poor must be treated fairly in the courts, neither receiving partiality (23:3) nor being cheated in lawsuits (23:6). Finally, the Sabbatical Year regulations require that the land is to be left fallow in the seventh year so that the poor may eat what grows naturally on the land, in the vineyard, and in the orchard (23:10–12).

The Law of the Tabernacle

Two more legal sections follow the Covenant Code in the book of Exodus. Chapters 25–31 detail the regulations on the priesthood and the building of the tabernacle, while chapters 35–40 report on the people's carrying out of the instructions to build the tabernacle. Both of these are preceded by narratives that keep the laws grounded in the story of the people: the first narrative (24:1–18) contains the covenant-making ceremony, while the second (32:1–34:35) records the incident of the golden calf and the restoration of the covenant.

The tabernacle was the movable shrine that housed the ark of the covenant, God's throne. The tabernacle was quite literally the center of the community as the Israelites wandered in the wilderness. According to Num 1:48–2:31, the tribes were to camp around the tabernacle, with three tribes camping on each of the four sides. The priests, all of whom were from the tribe of Levi, camped closest to the tabernacle, forming an inner circle surrounding the tabernacle on all sides. The tabernacle was the tent where Moses met with God, and it was to this tent that the people brought their offerings. It served as a precursor to the temple that would later be built by Solomon in Jerusalem and, not surprisingly, laid out according to the same plan.

> **Tabernacle:** a tent that housed the ark of the covenant during the wilderness period. It was a portable shrine built according to the same plan as the later temple in Jerusalem.

Exodus 25–27 describes the building of the tabernacle and each of the elements housed in it. The text goes into great—almost excruciating—detail, so these are not the most exciting chapters in the book of Exodus. But understanding the tabernacle is important for comprehending the religious life of the ancient Israelites, and it's not a good idea to ignore a topic to which the Scriptures give so much space.

Before the directions about the tabernacle itself, the text gives instructions for building the religious objects to be housed in it. Then Exod 25:10–22 describes the ark of the covenant. This ark, which formed the theological center of the tabernacle complex, was thought to be the throne of God. Its dimensions were approximately 1.25 meters long,

> **Ark of the covenant:** a gold-covered box that was viewed as the movable throne of God. In the wilderness period it was housed in the tabernacle. It was later moved into the inner sanctuary of the temple in Jerusalem by Solomon.

.75 meters wide, and .75 meters high (assuming a cubit equals half a meter). The lid of the ark, known as the mercy seat, was topped with two cherubim, and poles attached on each side carried the ark. (For a visual depiction of the ark, see the movie *Raiders of the Lost Ark*, in which the model of the ark is fairly accurate.) The presence of these two cherubim led to expressions such as that in Psalm 99:1: "The LORD is king; let the peoples tremble! He sits enthroned upon the cherubim; let the earth quake!"

This imagery occurs again in Isaiah 6, when the prophet Isaiah has a vision of God seated on his throne in the temple while the angels fly around singing the praises of God. The ark, as the movable throne, also lies behind Ezekiel's vision in Ezekiel 1, where God appears to him by the river Chebar in Babylon.

Other paraphernalia was required for the tabernacle as well. In Exod 25:23–30, Moses receives instructions for the table for the bread of the presence, the bread that was placed before the ark of the covenant inside the sanctuary. This is followed in 25:31–40 with a description of the seven-branched lamp stand, probably formed to represent the tree of life so common in ancient Near Eastern iconography. The olive oil used to fuel this lamp is prescribed in 27:20–21, and finally, 30:1–10 provides instructions for the incense altar. All of these items were for the inner sanctuary of the tabernacle. Two more installations, used in the outer court, were the wooden altar for sacrifice and the bronze basin described in 27:1–8 and 30:17–21, respectively.

Chapters 26 and 27 provide the layout for the tabernacle itself. It consisted of two parts, the inner sanctuary and the outer court. The inner sanctuary, which housed the ark of the covenant, measured 30 cubits (15 meters) long by 10 cubits (5 meters) wide. The curtains for the inner sanctuary were made from twisted linen of blue, purple, and crimson, with images of cherubim worked into the linen. These were attached to a wooden framework overlaid with gold and inserted into silver stands. The linen curtains were covered on the outside with a curtain of goat's hair and reddened ram's skins to form a tent over the sanctuary. A curtain divided the tent into two sections, the antechamber and the holy of holies (or most holy place). The ark resided in the holy of holies, while the antechamber contained the table for the bread of presence, the incense altar, and the seven-branched lamp stand.

The outer court of the tabernacle was a rectangular structure 100 cubits (50 meters) in length and 50 cubits (25 meters) in width. The court was entered through a doorway on the east end of the tent. The outer walls were placed around the inner sanctuary in such a way that the front of the sanctuary was at the centerline of the length of the outer court. This allowed the ark of the covenant to sit in the center of the western half of the tabernacle while the wooden altar for sacrifices sat in the center of the eastern half. The wooden altar was the place of sacrifice for the people of Israel. They were allowed to enter the outer court of the tabernacle, but only the priests could enter the inner sanctuary. This practice mirrors that of the later temple, where the sacrifices were done on the altar in the forecourt of the temple proper.

The description of the tabernacle presented here is greatly simplified from that in Exod 26–27, and I encourage you to try to make sense of the text in the Bible. Unfortunately, many of the terms used in this passage are technical terms whose meanings we don't completely understand. There are other difficulties too. For example, although the text goes into great detail to explain how each individual frame of the inner sanctuary was put together, it does not mention how the frames fit together with one another. Some scholars suggest that the frames overlapped, while others see them fitting end to end. The measurements stipulated for the different elements of the tabernacle also present some problems, as it is difficult to make them fit together with other given measurements. While these technical aspects don't affect our overall understanding of the function of the tabernacle, it is interesting to try to work out the details of how the tabernacle may have looked.

Conversations with the Law in Exodus

How can we use the laws in Exodus for life within the church today? For a couple of reasons, it is difficult to fit the biblical law to modern situations. The first factor is historical. Laws are always specific to the culture and time in which they are written, and the culture of Iron Age Israel was greatly different from our twenty-first-century culture. So biblical regulations on slavery are no more applicable today than our laws concerning vehicle emissions would have been in ancient Israel—we don't have slaves, and they didn't have cars. We obviously need to make adjustments to take these differences into consideration.

The other factor is theological. Not only are we separated from ancient Israel by more than two thousand years; we are also separated by the fact that the covenant of which the laws in Exodus are a part was not a covenant made with Gentiles. It was a covenant specifically with the Israelites. And while we have been grafted into Israel, as Paul argues in Romans 11:17–24, the church decided early in its history that the laws of the first covenant were not directly applicable to Gentile Christians. At the council in Acts 15, the early believers decided that Gentiles weren't required to follow the law, and they asked only that the Gentiles observe those laws which would allow them to be ritually pure so that the Jewish Christians—who were still following the law—could continue to be in fellowship with them.

The upshot of these two factors is that when we affirm the Old Testament law as the word of God—and the church has consistently held that it *is* the word of God for both Jewish and Gentile believers—we must appropriate it very carefully. In seeking to be faithful to the original text, we must be aware of the historical distance between us and ancient Israel while also cultivating a sensitivity to the cultures in which we seek to use the law today. And although determining how to use the law isn't easy under such conditions, it is still possible. Indeed, the process of reading contemporary issues in the light of the biblical laws can—and should—be theologically stimulating, drawing us into a deeper understanding of both the present and the past. Addressing current situations in the light of the biblical tradition can only enrich our comprehension of both.

Remember, the laws in Exodus weren't written in a vacuum or intended to be read apart from the narrative. They were grounded in the exodus event, the salvation of the people from Egypt. The laws were not intended to be understood as eternal, unchangeable statements of the divine will. In delivering the people from Egypt, God constituted a people for God's own, and the

The laws were grounded in the exodus event, the salvation of the people from Egypt.

laws that formed the people into a community reflect that fact. The stipulations in Exodus provide the pattern of life for the people of Israel. Their function is not so much to tell the people how to act as to show them what it means to be the people of God. In that sense, the laws are more than mere rules. They are the foundation of the faith community.

When we use the Book of the Covenant as a faith community today, we must follow the same model. Strict, literal adherence to the regulations and stipulations robs the law of its power to form the people of God. It is important instead to focus on the patterns of life that the law puts forth.

Take the law concerning a daughter sold as a slave in Exod 21:7–11, for example. Although the idea of selling anyone, especially one's own offspring, into slavery is unacceptable within the church—as is the idea that a father would have such absolute power over his daughter—the pattern established in this law is clear. The woman isn't property, and the slave owner isn't free to do whatever he wants with her. He must treat her fairly, whether he marries her himself (which is the assumption made by the law) or allows his son to marry her. If he doesn't like her, he isn't free to sell her; her family must be allowed to redeem her. And if he takes a second wife, the slave is still to have the honor and privileges of a first wife. Furthermore, violation of this law automatically gives the slave her freedom.

As Christians, of course, we must always read these laws in the light of Jesus' statement that all of the law and prophets hang on the two laws to love God and love our neighbors as ourselves (Matt 22:34–40). This may require us to go beyond the law, but it will never require of us less than what is in the law. In the case of the daughter sold into slavery (Exod 21:7–11), while we wouldn't allow a daughter to be sold into slavery in modern times, the fact that the woman cannot be treated as property and must be given the rights of a wife must be upheld. Asking how such laws fulfill the requirement to love our neighbors as ourselves provides a lens through which to view these laws. Seen in this light, this law, which on the surface seems to promote the subjugation of women through slavery, is actually a call to recognize the personhood of all people, both male and female. In acknowledging that this law forbids the woman to be treated as property, we are invited to examine our attitudes about women today to see if there are still ways women are treated as property or objects.

Just as the Book of the Covenant is rooted in the life of ancient Israel, so is the law of the tabernacle. Obviously, the tabernacle was intended for a specific period in the life of the Israelites, and we are not expected to reconstruct the tabernacle today. Yet the picture of the tabernacle at the center of the Israelite camp during the time in the wilderness shows that worship is still central in our lives today. The message of the tabernacle is that God is most present when we come together as a congregation in the act of worship. As important as education, social ministry, personal spirituality, and other facets of our faith life are, they are secondary to our worship as a community. It is in this worship that God forms us and renews us for these other areas of ministry and work.

Because of this, we must pay special attention to the care Exodus takes when providing the instructions for the building of the tabernacle. This is not a random building that the people are free to design as they choose. Instead, the tabernacle is to be the dwelling place of God and the meeting point between God and humanity, and each element of it is designed with that purpose in mind.

Every church building committee should be required to read the description of the construction of the tabernacle in Exodus before they begin planning a church sanctuary. This is not because they should duplicate the details of the tabernacle in the church but rather because the building they have been called to design is to be at the center of the life of the church community. It will be, quite literally, the place where God and the people meet. Just as the tabernacle was designed with that purpose in mind, so must our places of worship be constructed to serve that end. Although we must always remember that the people, not the building, are the church, this doesn't mean that the building is unimportant. The Israelites, formed into a people at Mount Sinai, were very aware of this fact, yet they took great care in the construction of the tabernacle. Their story should call us to the same care when building our places of worship. The exact details of the architecture of the tabernacle may not be important, but the overall message is.

A Pattern for Living

The laws in the book of Exodus provided the ancient Israelites with the pattern of living that was to characterize the people of God. Far from being laws covering only religious matters, the laws in Exodus show God's concern for all areas of life. Within the faith community, *everything* is within God's purview. Every aspect matters to the life of faith, from the lowliest cow that has fallen into a pit to the grand construction of God's dwelling place. And while historical and theological distance prevents these laws from functioning in the life of the modern church in the same way they did in ancient Israel, they still speak today, giving us the patterns of life that form and inform us as the people of God.

CHAPTER THREE

Sacrifices in Leviticus

If someone were to draw up a list of sections in the Bible that Christians consider to be the least relevant for today, the description of sacrifices in Lev 1–7 would certainly be somewhere near the top. This passage would also top a list of texts that Christians consider the most boring to read—surpassed perhaps only by the seemingly endless genealogies in the Old Testament. And its place near the top of these two lists accounts for the fact that Lev 1–7—the discussion of offerings in the temple—ranks among the least-read sections of the Old Testament.

We can't do much to make Lev 1–7 more exciting. After all, how many people care precisely what part of the entrails should be washed before being burnt (Lev 1:9)? But the fact that this passage is so little understood within the church is lamentable, because understanding these sacrifices[1] helps us understand many parts of the Old Testament—and some parts of the New Testament too. For instance, one of the primary metaphors used in the New Testament to describe the death of Jesus Christ is that of sacrifice (Rom 3:25; Eph 5:2; Heb 9:26; 1 John 4:10), and the understanding of sacrifice that the New Testament writers had was informed by Lev 1–7.

In addition, the sacrifices described in Leviticus were the central act of communal worship in the ancient Israelite community. They are, in fact, the sacraments of the Old Testament. To understand the worship of the Israelites, therefore, we must come to terms with the sacrifices. To try to explore their worship without knowing about the sacrifices would be like trying to understand Christian worship without knowing about the Eucharist—sacrifice was central to the Israelites' understanding of what it meant to follow God.

The Five Sacrifices

Leviticus 1–7 provides a description of five sacrifices:

- the burnt offering
- the grain offering
- the offering of well-being
- the sin offering
- the guilt offering

These are the titles applied to the sacrifices by the NRSV, but as we'll see, some of the names are slightly mistranslated. The description of the sacrifices is divided into two sections. After an introduction to the book of Leviticus in 1:1–2, Lev 1:3–6:7 describes the offering from the point of view of the person who actually makes the offering. It explains when the people should bring their offerings as well as what animals or grains are acceptable. The second section, Lev 6:8–7:38, describes the offerings from the perspective of the priests' responsibilities. This section provides specific instructions for how priests are to perform each of the sacrifices as well as the ritual actions that accompany them.

Offerand: the person who brings the offering

In studying the sacrifices, it is helpful to pay attention to who is doing the offering, what part of the animal or grain is offered, and what is done with the part of the offering not given to God. Sometimes the priests do the offering; at other times the person bringing the offering—called the offerand—does it.

Sometimes the entire offering is given to God; at other times only part of it is. And the leftover part of the offering (if any) sometimes goes to the priest and sometimes goes to the offerand. But the most important thing to notice about each sacrifice is the purpose for which it is offered.

Although the sacrifices in Leviticus were used primarily within the land of Israel, the book of Leviticus is set as God's speech to Moses while the congregation of Israel was still at Mount Sinai. So the instructions for these offerings specify that the correct place for the offering was the tabernacle. Once the temple had been built in Jerusalem, however, the temple became the focus of the sacrificial act.

THE BURNT OFFERING

The first offering (Lev 1:3–17) is the burnt offering, also known as the whole offering. This is the holiest of all offerings prescribed for the Israelites. At first, the prescribed sacrifice was a male bull, but later, other animals, including sheep, goats, and birds, were substituted. These smaller animals were probably included to make provision for those who couldn't afford an entire bull. But no matter what the animal, it had to be a male without blemish. Animals with some kind of defect were not acceptable offerings, for a perfect God requires perfect sacrifices. This idea is reflected in Mal 1:6–8, where the prophet chides the people for bringing imperfect offerings. If an earthly ruler would not accept blemished offerings, he asks, why should God?

The offerand brought the animal to the entrance to the tabernacle, the meeting place between God and humanity. He placed his hand on the animal to signify his ownership,[2] then killed and skinned the animal, then dashed its blood against the side of the altar to avoid guilt for the shedding of blood. After the offerand had washed the entrails to remove impurity, the priest burned the entire animal on the altar. This is one of the sacrifices in which the offerand participated in the offering by doing all the killing and preparation. Only when the animal was to be placed on the altar did the priest take over.

The description of this sacrifice includes a phrase that occurs in each of the descriptions of the offerings. Leviticus 1:9 says that the offering is turned into "smoke on the altar as . . . a pleasing odor to the LORD." This clearly distinguishes the Israelite idea of sacrifice from that of cultures around them. In Mesopotamia, for example, the sacrifice was seen as providing food for the gods. Although a few verses in the Old Testament point to this meaning of the sacrifices (e.g., Num 28:2), in Leviticus it is ruled out completely. God is never said to eat the sacrifices. Instead, God is merely pleased with the odor of the burning meat and grain.

The burnt offering was the main type of sacrifice in ancient Israel, as a search of the Old Testament makes clear. The Hebrew Bible contains over 250 references to the burnt offering, even prior to the institution of the covenant at Mount Sinai. Noah offered a burnt offering after being delivered from the flood (Gen 8:20). Abraham was commanded to kill his son Isaac as a burnt offering, although a ram was later provided in Isaac's place (Gen 22). Jethro, Moses' father-in-law, a non-Israelite, also made burnt offerings prior to the Israelites' arrival at Mount Sinai (Exod 18:12). The burnt offering wasn't limited to Israel but was common in the ancient Near East. It could be used for a number of purposes, although worship, thanksgiving, and the petitioning of God seem to be the primary uses.

THE GRAIN OFFERING

The second sacrifice is the grain offering, described in Lev 2:1–16. The grain offering could have been used as a substitute for the burnt offering—if a person were too poor to bring even a small bird for the burnt offering, some scholars argue, the grain offering could have been used in its place. It is not entirely clear, however, that this is the case. Whereas the burnt offering was completely burned on the altar, only a small part of the grain offering was given to God. The rest was given to the priests. Since the purpose of the grain offering isn't stated, it is difficult to determine how much it has in common with the burnt offering.

The Bible describes three different types of grain offerings: the unbaked grain, the baked grain, and the firstfruits. The unbaked grain was to be mixed with oil and frankincense, while the baked grain was to have oil spread on it. The firstfruit offering was to be roasted grain, also mixed with oil and frankincense. As in the case of the burnt offering, the offerand did the preparation. The priest took over only when it was time to place the grain on the fire on the altar.

THE OFFERING OF WELL-BEING

The third sacrifice is the offering of well-being, covered in chapter 3 of Leviticus. This offering is sometimes called a peace offering, as the title of this offering is derived from the Hebrew word *shalom*, which means "peace, health, well-being." The well-being offering is the only voluntary sacrifice in Lev 1–7. While the other sacrifices made atonement for sins and purified the offerand and the tabernacle/temple, the well-being offering was given because the offerand wanted to show thankfulness to the Lord. It could be used when a vow was fulfilled or as a freewill offering (Lev 22:21) or as a thanksgiving on any occasion.

Shalom: the Hebrew word for "peace and well-being."

Unlike the burnt offering, which was entirely given to God, and the grain offering, part of which went to God and part to the priests, the sacrifice of well-being was mostly the property of the offerand. Several parts of the animal had to be removed and burnt as an offering to God. These included the fat around the entrails (technically called "suet"), both kidneys, and the appendage (tail) of the liver. Fat was given to God because it was considered to be the choice part of the animal. According to Lev 3:16, "all fat is the LORD's" and is not to be eaten.[3] The appendage of the liver was probably removed to avoid confusion with the Mesopotamian rituals of divination that used this appendage to determine the will of the god (a practice known as heptoscopy). Clay models of livers have been unearthed in Mesopotamia. These clay livers include inscriptions that interpret deformities in certain parts of the liver. By using the clay livers as a guide, priests could interpret the liver of the sacrificed animal and deliver an oracle to the offerand. One of the principal areas of the liver used for divination was the appendage. Since divination was forbidden in Israel (Deut 18:10), the practice of removing the appendage safeguarded the offerand from such charges.

To understand the offering of well-being, remember that the killing of any animal in ancient Israel was considered an offering. Anyone who killed an animal in any place other than the tabernacle, a shrine, or the temple was guilty of shedding blood (Lev 17:1–7). So any time people wanted to eat meat, they had to offer a sacrifice. Meat formed a very small part of the diet in the ancient Near East, and with the exception of royalty, most people ate meat only on occasions of celebration, which corresponded with well-being sacrifice offered in thanksgiving. The well-being offering was brought to the temple for sacrifice, then taken back to the offerand's house, where it was used in the feast. In this way, the people included God in their celebrations.

THE SIN OFFERING

Although the name of the sin offering, described in Lev 4:1–5:13, is derived from the Hebrew root that means "sin," the form of the word carries the meaning of "cleansing." So a better designation for this offering would be the purification offering—and that is how this offering functioned. It provided forgiveness for the offerand, but more importantly, it cleansed the tabernacle or temple. Although individual impurity was problematic, more serious were the sins and other contaminants that made the temple impure. Whenever these sins were committed, the offender was to bring an offering to the temple to purify it.

The temple needed to be holy because God, who is holy and who was thought to reside in the temple, cannot dwell in an impure place. And while small amounts of impurity were allowed as long as offerings were made in due time, when the sins of the people became too numerous, the temple became unfit for God's presence. This is how the prophet Ezekiel interpreted the destruction of the Jerusalem temple in 587 BCE. He claimed that the temple had become too polluted for God to live there, so the glory of God departed from the temple and allowed the Babylonians to destroy it (Ezek 8–11).

The need for purity explains why the purification offering and the guilt offering were mandatory sacrifices, in contrast to the burnt offering, the grain offering, and the offering of well-being, all of which were voluntary. The voluntary offerings were made to God in thankfulness or worship. These final two offerings, however, were needed to keep the temple in working order so that God might continue to dwell in the midst of the people. The people themselves also had to be purified, as God dwelled in their midst. For someone who was impure to come into contact with that which was holy was dangerous. The maintenance of purity, therefore, was also the maintenance of the safety of the community.

The instructions for the purification offering differ according to the sinner. There were four different classes—the priest, the whole congregation, the king, and individuals—with a specific type of animal for each class. The priest had to offer a bull. The same offering was mandated in cases when the entire community sinned. The ruler had to bring a male goat, while an individual was to bring a female goat or sheep. In addition, different parts of the tabernacle were sprinkled with the blood in each case. For the priest's sacrifice, some of the blood was sprinkled on the altar of incense inside the inner sanctuary of the tent of meeting. Additional blood was sprinkled in front of the curtain that hid the ark of the covenant. For the congregation's sacrifice, some of the blood was sprinkled before the curtain, but none was put on the incense altar. For the sacrifices of the king and individuals, some blood was used to anoint the horns at the corner of the altar of burnt offering. In all four cases, the remainder of the blood was poured out at the base of the altar of burnt offering.

The reasoning behind the different locations for the sprinkled blood had to do with the severity of the contamination of the altar. Obviously, the priests had the most contact with the tabernacle, so it's not surprising that the blood of their sacrifice was sprinkled in the inner sanctuary. The same was done for the sacrifice of the entire congregation, as sins by the whole community brought high levels of impurity. What is interesting is that the king and other individuals both had the blood of their offerings sprinkled in the outer court. We might have suspected that the sins of the king would be considered more dangerous than those of common people, but that was not the case. The only difference between the royal and common sacrifices was that the king's offering had to be male, while the people could bring a female.

After the animal had been killed and its blood sprinkled in the appropriate place to make atonement for the sanctuary, the priest prepared the animal just as he did for the sacrifice of well-being. He removed all the fat, as well as other parts of the kidneys and liver, and then burned it on the altar. In the case of the offering for a priest or the whole congregation, the remainder of the animal was taken outside the camp and burned. Neither the priests nor the people were to eat of this sacrifice. One possible explanation for this is that the impurity of the temple had been transferred to the animal. Once that occurred, the animal was not appropriate for an offering in the tabernacle. The impurity would also make it unfit to eat. The animal had to be burned outside the camp to prevent its impurity from contaminating the people further. In the case of the offering for a king or an individual, however, the animal was to be eaten by the priests, since its blood had not entered the inner sanctuary (Lev 6:24–30).

Interestingly, the instructions for this and the following sacrifice applied only to unintentional sins—no sacrifice was provided for intentional sins. And Num 15:27–31 stipulates that those who committed intentional sins were to be cut off from the people of God. They had to continue to bear their guilt.

But Hebrew Scriptures scholar Jacob Milgrom disagrees with this explanation. He points out that four texts in the Old Testament, each of which deals with intentional sins (Lev 5:5; 16:21; 26:40; Num 5:7), require confession before the sacrifice. Milgrom suggests that confession is the means by which intentional sins are turned into unintentional sins.[4] This idea corresponds to the Christian notion that repentance is necessary before forgiveness is possible.

THE GUILT OFFERING

The final offering is the guilt offering, also called the restitution or reparation offering. This sacrifice, closely related to the purification offering, is covered in Lev 5:14–6:7. It was performed in the same way as the purification offering, with the exception that any priest could eat it. Three cases are given in which a person had to offer a guilt offering: sinning against a holy item, committing an unknown sin, and swearing falsely in a matter concerning money. In each of these cases, restitution had to be made. The offering was brought to the tabernacle or temple, and its value was calculated before the animal was slaughtered. The animal itself was enough for atonement in the case of unknown sins, but in the case of sins against holy items or false oaths, additional reparations had to be made. For sins against holy items, 20 percent of the value of the lamb was added in silver, and the money was given to the temple. For false oaths, the original money had to be returned to the injured party, along with an additional 20 percent as a penalty.

Table 1 shows the distribution of who was allowed to eat of the various sacrifices and how much God received of each offering. God received at least a portion of each of the offerings, while the remainder was either destroyed, kept by the priests, or given back to the offerand. While it may seem odd that the priests kept major portions of the offering, this was their only means of making a living. Unlike the rest of the tribes, the Levites were not given land, so they had to receive their living from their work in the temple. Since they received no monetary wages for their work, the receipt of offerings was their only source of income. Although such a system could be abused, as the prophet Hosea pointed out (Hos 4:8), it did provide payment to those who looked after the religious needs of the people.

Conversations with the Sacrifices

Many Christians believe that the Old Testament sacrifices were performed primarily to allow God—or to cause God—to forgive the Israelites when they had sinned. We tend to take this view because when the New Testament authors described Christ as a sacrifice, they were drawing a metaphorical connection between the work of Christ and the purification offering described in Leviticus. We often think of

TABLE 1

	God	Priests	Offerand
Burnt offering	All		
Grain offering	Portion	Remainder	
Well-being offering	Portion		Remainder
Purification offering	Portion	Remainder*	
Guilt offering	Portion	Remainder	

*In cases in which the blood was not brought into the inner sanctuary.

the Old Testament sacrificial system as an arrangement that worked fine until Jesus came but became unnecessary once he arrived.

But our survey of the types of sacrifices in Leviticus should show that while there is some truth to this understanding of the offerings, it doesn't do justice to the purpose and place of the offerings in the life of ancient Israel. First and foremost, only two of the sacrifices in Leviticus were designed with the forgiveness of sins in mind: the purification offering and the guilt offering. And though these were concerned with sin, it was mainly the cleansing of the temple that was accomplished through these offerings. Forgiveness was only a secondary part of the sacrifice. In addition, the guilt offering was used only in three unusual cases, which means that only the purification offering was used regularly.

So the majority of sacrifices that were offered were both voluntary and unconnected to the forgiveness of sin. The burnt offering, the grain offering, and the offering of well-bring were all expressions of worship used either to give thanks to God (offering of well-being) or to make petitions to God (burnt and grain offerings). They weren't mandatory, and it was up to the offerand to decide when to bring them. Because of this, the sacrifices should not be seen as merely a way to placate the deity but as a central part of all types of worship.

LEVITICUS AND THE CHURCH TODAY

Few books have attempted to deal with the issue of how Leviticus can be heard as Scripture within the contemporary church. One of the few recent books that has addressed this issue is Allen P. Ross's book *Holiness to the Lord*.[5] Ross does a good job of engaging many of the problems. Although Ross tends to spiritualize the reading of the text too much, his book provides rewarding insights. But as one reviewer, Samuel E. Balentine, points out, although Leviticus is full of ritual and worship, Ross never deals with the ritual aspects of the text. Balentine notes that Ross has "shed some light on Israel's *theology* of sacrifice, priestly service, atonement, and so on, but he has offered little help on how contemporary worshipers may *enact this theology* through appropriate rituals that engage both body and mind."[6] This oversight may, in part, be due to Ross's location within the evangelical tradition, a tradition in which worship is more spontaneous than and not as liturgical as worship in other traditions. Those of us within the churches of the Anglican Communion, however, may be in a better position to examine the important issue of ritual.

Ritual is important because it is the way we act out our theology. Whether in ancient Israel or in the modern church, ritual is never done merely with the mind, and it should never be separated from its meaning. It must engage the entire believer— mind and body—in communion with God. And it is in worship where our theology is most deeply expressed. The sacrifices are essentially the sacraments of the Israelites—ways of receiving God's grace. So if we want to apply the book of Leviticus to the modern church, let's look for the parallels between our worship and the worship of the ancient Israelites. As we come to understand their worship, we come to understand our own much more deeply.

Ritual is important because it is the way we act out our theology.

They offered sacrifices on all occasions of life. For the Hebrew people, worship wasn't a once-a-week obligation limited to a specific day. They didn't worship only when they needed help, as if God were a celestial parent who got them out of trouble. Instead, they worshiped to express both happiness and sadness, need and need fulfilled, petition and thankfulness for answered prayers. They incorporated all facets of life into the community's worship, which in turn led them to see God involved in all areas of their lives. Worship isn't just about praising God but about presenting our entire existence to God and learning that the Lord is present in both joy and suffering. The ancient Israelites understood that worship isn't one-dimensional.

As such, the sacrifices complement the other aspect of worship that we have preserved in the Old Testament, the psalms. If the offerings were the physical acts associated with worship, the psalms provided the soundtrack. Many of the psalms are associated with liturgical actions, and some even speak directly of sacrifice. Psalm 66:13–15, for instance, mentions a number of the offerings found in Leviticus:

I will come into your house with burnt offerings; I will pay you my vows, those that my lips uttered and my mouth promised when I was in trouble. —Ps 66:13–15

I will come into your house with burnt offerings;
   I will pay you my vows,
those that my lips uttered
   and my mouth promised when I was in trouble.
I will offer to you burnt offerings of fatlings,
   with the smoke of the sacrifice of rams;
I will make an offering of bulls and goats.

And just as the sacrifices deal with a number of situations, so do the psalms. There are psalms of praise (both individual and communal), psalms of petition (both individual and communal), songs of thanksgiving, and psalms for particular religious festivals.

Both the community and individuals were required to make sacrifices. The burnt offering could be offered on behalf of the entire congregation or for specific individuals. And the purification offering provided for cases of both communal and individual sins. This calls us to recognize that our relationship with God isn't just an individual matter. We belong to the community, and we are the people of God most clearly when we come together as a congregation. But there is a parallel risk as well. If on the one side the danger is that we'll be too individualistic, the danger on the other side is that we'll allow the community to be religious on our behalf. Sometimes we're prone to believe that belonging to a worshiping community is enough, releasing us from individual responsibility. The sacrifices in Leviticus contradict this perspective. They point us in both directions, calling us to fulfill our individual and corporate responsibilities as the people of God.

In the Western world, of the two extremes mentioned here, we have a tendency to go toward the more individualistic side, not only in our worship but in our understanding of sin. We're much more willing to admit our wrongdoings as individuals than we are to notice the sinful things we're doing as a society. It is important that we pay attention to the corporate side of sin to which Leviticus draws our attention. Whether this sin involves our parish, our denomination, or our nation, we must be willing to acknowledge our sins and ask for forgiveness, especially since these corporate sins are the ones that can do the most damage to others. The perils of corporate sin outweigh those of individual misdeeds, which is probably why Leviticus gives instruction for the purification offering for the entire community before it gives instructions for individuals.

Our worship is connected to the forgiveness of our sins. The Israelites made the purification offering so that they might continue to worship in the presence of a holy God. Impurity, the opposite of holiness, was a danger to the worshiper. Approaching a holy God while being impure was risky. An illustration of this danger is found in 2 Sam 6:1–11. When David moved the ark of the covenant—the holiest object in Israel—to Jerusalem, he did so by placing the ark on a cart pulled by oxen. When the oxen stumbled, one of the drivers, a man named Uzzah, reached out and touched the ark to prevent it from falling off the cart. But because Uzzah was impure, his contact with the holy brought about his death. In the same way, Israelites who drew near to the sanctuary were drawing near to the holy, for they believed that God literally dwelled in the temple.

The church has also recognized the importance of holiness within the worship service, stressing it at times to greater and lesser degrees. Both major forms of worship in the Anglican Church—the Eucharistic service and the prayer office—contain occasions for the confession of sin. In the morning and evening prayer services, this occasion comes at the beginning of the service to stress that we need to repent as we draw near to God. In the Eucharist, the confession and absolution come between the service of the word and the service of the table. Because the bread and wine are seen as the presence of Christ in the service, the confession prepares us to draw closer to God as we approach the altar. If we are to apply the ideas of Lev 1–7 to our own worship, we need to remind ourselves to see the service as an interaction with God and remember that such times require us to be pure.

The final sacrifice, the guilt offering, carried with it the necessity of making restitution to the injured party. Although the Old Testament offerings are not usually thought to bring reconciliation between people, this is exactly how the guilt offering functioned. In addition to receiving God's forgiveness, we need to make amends for the harm we've done to others. Jesus certainly recognized the ongoing importance of such a sacrifice, even when others focused merely on the rit-

So when you are offering
your gift at the altar, if you
remember that your brother
or sister has something
against you, leave your gift
there before the altar and
go; first be reconciled to
your brother or sister, and
then come and offer your
gift." —Matt 5:23–24

ual's bringing forgiveness. In the Sermon on the Mount, he says, "So when you are offering your gift at the altar, if you remember that your brother or sister has something against you, leave your gift there before the altar and go; first be reconciled to your brother or sister, and then come and offer your gift" (Matt 5:23–24). Although he doesn't deny the significance of the sacrifice, he reinforces the fact that mending the relationship is also important. Just as sin against God creates a barrier to worship, so does an injured relationship with another Christian. The guilt offering of the Israelites reminds us that true worship of God requires us to be reconciled to God as well as our neighbor.

From Sacrifice to Offering

Across the millennia, the Hebrew understanding of worship continues to inform our worship as Christians. The burnt sacrifice, the grain offering, the sacrifice of well-being, the purification offering, and the guilt offering—the least-read passages in the Bible—all deserve our creative attention in the church.

The discussion of how the sacrifices inform our ideas of worship in the modern church is by no means exhaustive. No attempt has been made to cover all areas on which Lev 1–7 sheds light, since no study could ever deplete the richness of these passages. Instead, the ideas given here are meant to be suggestive, and the reader is certainly encouraged to explore the topic more fully. At its best, all theology is creative, and creativity is certainly called for here. The burnt sacrifice, the grain offering, the sacrifice of well-being, the purification offering, and the guilt offering all deserve more attention in the church, and I hope this chapter will invite Christians to move Lev 1–7 off the list of least-read passages in the Bible.

CHAPTER FOUR

The Law in Leviticus

If the sacrificial laws of Leviticus top the chart of least-read sections of the Bible, the rest of Leviticus isn't far behind. We don't turn to it for comfort in times of trouble or crisis. It's not read for devotional study or quoted on greeting cards. And Christians rarely think of Leviticus when they want to solve theological or ethical problems. In short, Leviticus is simply not on most people's radar screens.

Even among Christian biblical scholars, Leviticus is problematic. For biblical commentaries aimed at a Christian audience, it isn't unusual for Leviticus to be one of the last books of the Bible to be covered. Leviticus is even neglected in the church's worship. The Episcopal Church's lectionary, for example, lists Leviticus only twice in the three-year-cycle of Sunday Scripture readings. One is on the fifth Sunday of Easter in Year C, when it's offered as an alternate reading,

Commentaries: books that discuss the interpretation of individual books of the Bible. Commentaries provide a verse-by-verse explanation of the meaning of the text.

Lectionary: a list that provides four readings to be read in services in the church: an Old Testament reading, a psalm, a New Testament epistle reading, and a Gospel reading. Most Sunday lectionaries repeat on a three-year cycle.

Proper: the Sundays during Ordinary Time on the church calendar are called Propers.

used only if the church decides not to follow the practice of reading from Acts in place of the Old Testament passage during Easter. Since most churches do read Acts, this reading is almost never used. The other occurrence is on Proper 2 of Year A, used when Easter falls very early in the year—which doesn't happen very often.

The Church and Leviticus

The problem of Leviticus in the church exists for a couple of reasons. The first reason is historical, since the laws were intended for a particular time and place. The rules of ancient Babylon, for instance—with no provisions for dealing with such modern matters as motorized traffic, air travel, and the Internet—wouldn't suffice to govern our lives today. By the same token, our laws wouldn't provide for order in ancient Babylon, since few modern states have rules on the books stipulating how the next high priest of Marduk is to be chosen or how fast you can drive your chariot. The laws in Leviticus are no different. They are set in the Israel of the first millennium BCE, not England, Canada, or the United States in the twenty-first century CE. When we try to use Leviticus to address contemporary issues, we're faced with the problem of overcoming a 2,500-year time gap and vastly different cultural and geographical settings.

Babylon: a kingdom in the ancient Near East centered in the area of modern Iraq. The Neo-Babylonian Empire controlled the ancient Near East, including Israel, from 614 to 538 BCE.

Marduk: the chief god of Babylon.

The theological problems with using Leviticus are just as acute—as the first Christians quickly discovered. Early in the church's history, leaders had to decide whether Gentile converts to Christianity should follow the Jewish law. Christianity began as a Jewish religion, but as it spread within the Roman Empire, more and more Gentiles joined. Acts 15 describes a council called in the early church to discuss the problem. Its decision, presented by James, was that while Gentiles didn't have to follow the law, they were to "abstain only from things polluted by idols and from fornication and from whatever has been strangled and from blood" (Acts 15:20). These stipulations, all of which concern purity, were kept to maintain fellowship between Jewish Christians and non-Jewish believers.

What of the rest of the law? Nothing is said. But it is clear that in the New Testament, biblical authors were quick to use the law to support their positions. For example, Paul quotes from laws found in Lev 18:5; Deut 21:23; and Deut 27:36 to prove his point in Gal 3:10–14. In 1 Tim 1:8 Paul asserts that "the law is good, if one uses it legitimately." James tells us that we do well if we follow the commandment to "love your neighbor as yourself" (Jas 2:8, quoting Lev 19:18). And Jesus, in the Sermon on the Mount, clearly states the importance of the law:

> The law is good, if one uses it legitimately. —1 Tim 1:8

"Do not think that I have come to abolish the law or the prophets; I have come not to abolish but to fulfill. For truly I tell you, until heaven and earth pass away, not one letter, not one stroke of a letter, will pass from the law until all is accomplished. Therefore, whoever breaks one of the least of these commandments, and teaches others to do the same, will be called least in the kingdom of heaven; but whoever does them and teaches them will be called great in the kingdom of heaven. For I tell you, unless your righteousness exceeds that of the scribes and Pharisees, you will never enter the kingdom of heaven." (Matt 5:17–20)

> "Do not think that I have come to abolish the law or the prophets; I have come not to abolish but to fulfill." —Matt 5:17

Despite the Council of Jerusalem's decision that observance of the law wasn't to be imposed on Gentiles, the law was clearly of continuing value for the early church.

So the theological challenge in using the law is to find a way between two extremes. The first extreme is to require a strict obedience to the law. On this side of the issue are those who say that every letter of the law must be followed exactly as it is written, ignoring the historical and theological problems inherent in that position. While few would accept such an absolute position on the law in all cases, many people do have a tendency toward this pole. For example, anytime you simply quote a law from the Old Testament to support an ethical position, you're using an absolutist approach. But a "God said it; that settles it" use of Scripture is problematic. At the other end of the spectrum are those

> **Council of Jerusalem:** an early church council that met in Jerusalem to discuss the issue of Gentiles becoming Christian. The council is recorded in Acts 15.

49

who, consciously or unconsciously, ignore the Old Testament law entirely, seeing it as irrelevant. Using the law this way surely runs afoul of Jesus' assertion that he hasn't come to abolish the law.

Happily, some scholars have tried to find a way to understand the law that steers a middle course between these two extremes. One common way is to categorize the laws according to some abstract principle. According to the practitioners of this method, we can distinguish between those laws that should be followed today and those we can safely ignore.

Consider, for example, the approach in the book *How to Read the Bible for All Its Worth* by Gordon Fee and Douglas Stuart.[1] In their chapter on interpreting the Old Testament law, they write, "The portion of laws from the Pentateuch that no longer apply to Christians can be grouped conveniently into two categories: (1) the Israelite *civil laws* and (2) the Israelite *ritual laws*. While some Old Testament laws still apply to us . . . these do not."[2] Other laws, which they categorize as *ethical*, are still applicable in the church. According to these scholars, these laws are in force because they are renewed within the New Testament. In other words, Old Testament laws still count if they have been repeated in the New Testament.

Although Fee and Stuart set out a contemporary statement of this approach, it is by no means new. It's even enshrined in the Thirtynine Articles of the Anglican faith. Article VII states, "Although the Law given from God by Moses, as touching Ceremonies and Rites, do not bind Christian men, nor the Civil precepts thereof ought of necessity to be received in any commonwealth; yet notwithstanding, no Christian man whatsoever is free from the obedience of the Commandments which are called Moral."[3]

Thirty-nine Articles: A statement of beliefs and practices adopted by the Episcopal church at its 1801 convention. It contains thirty-nine items addressing faith and practice. They are also called the Articles of Religion. They may be found in the historical documents section in the back of the Book of Common Prayer.

This four-hundred-year-old system still shapes the way Anglicans use the book of Leviticus. Even on the rare occasions that Lev 19:1–18 is read as part of the Sunday lectionary, many of the verses in that passage are omitted. A reading of the complete passage shows that the verses that have been left out are the ones that deal with civil and ritual law, while the verses that remain cover moral laws.

But this system doesn't do justice to the material in Leviticus. To find a system that works, we must first be familiar with the text itself. Perhaps the book of Leviticus can provide us with its own suggestions for how we could use it.

Ordination, Purity, and the Holiness Code

After the section on sacrifice in the first seven chapters, the law in Leviticus recounts the ordination of Aaron and his sons as priests in chapters 8–10. Here readers also will learn about the consecration of the tabernacle, constructed at the end of Exodus. The ordination process takes seven days and includes a number of sacrifices, among them purification offerings and burnt offerings, as well as the ordination sacrifice and an elevation offering. These last two aren't mentioned by name in Lev 1–7, but they may be variants on the offering of well-being and the grain offering. Blood is sprinkled on the tabernacle to purify it, and the priests are consecrated by having blood smeared on their right earlobes, their right thumbs, and their right big toes. The celebration ends on the eighth day, with Aaron and his sons offering sacrifices for themselves and the entire congregation. Chapter 10 continues with an account of two of Aaron's sons being struck down for incorrectly offering incense before the Lord.

The next section, Lev 11–15, deals with issues of purity within the community. Perhaps the best known of these laws are those dealing with animals that may and may not be eaten—the kosher laws. Scholars have numerous theories explaining why some animals are clean while others are unclean. Some scholars think some of the laws may have prohibited eating food associated with the religious practices of neighboring cultures. Others suggest that health reasons were the basis of the prohibitions. Each of these theories falls short, however, because neither explains all the cases. For example, while the prohibition against eating pork would protect against diseases such as trichinosis, other forbidden animals have no such health concerns attached to them.

Kosher: a word to describe food that may be eaten by Jews. Leviticus and Deuteronomy contain lists of the rules that determine whether a particular food is kosher.

The theory that best explains the food laws roots the distinction between clean and unclean animals in creation. The Priestly writer who codified the laws in their present form is also responsible for the creation account in Genesis 1. There God divided the world into three separate spheres on the first three days: water, sky, and land. On the following three days, God created the animals that inhabit each of these areas. God made some animals for food, while others could not be eaten. Sometimes physical signs indicated which animals could be eaten, while other times the behavior of the animal indicated its status. For the Priestly writer, everything in the universes had a place, and anything that didn't act according to the rules of its realm was dangerous.

Several examples make this clear. Leviticus 11:9–12 specifies which water animals could be eaten. This passage provides physical signs by which the Israelites could tell which animals were clean: only those animals that have fins and scales. Lobsters, for instance, with neither fins nor scales, were considered unclean. The reasoning? While a lobster lives in the water, it doesn't behave like a water creature. It walks rather than swims, making it suspect to the Priestly writer. Among birds, a similar reasoning holds. According to Lev 11:15, the ostrich isn't fit to be eaten because, though it's a bird, it can't fly. A stork, on the other hand, can fly but is still considered unclean in Lev 11:19. When the stork is in the sky, it flies as it should, but in the water it walks—inappropriate behavior for the realm of water. And more than that, it walks on the edge of the water, the boundary between land and sea. Boundaries are dangerous places according to the Priestly writer, so storks, by virtue of their boundary existence, should be avoided.

The remainder of Lev 11–15 deals with issues of cleanliness as well. Chapter 12 provides instructions for the way a woman was to be cleansed after giving birth. A male child caused the mother to be unclean for a week, while a female child caused two weeks of uncleanness. Both a burnt offering and a purification offering had to be offered at the end of this period. Chapters 13–15 deal with various skin diseases that made one unclean. These skin diseases, lumped together under the term "leprosy," were not the same as current-day leprosy, which is known as Hansen's Disease. Instead, it could refer to many kinds of skin ailments. (Mildew was also considered to be leprosy, although a type that affected houses.) All forms of leprosy were to be diagnosed by a priest to determine the extent and duration of uncleanness they caused. These laws seem particularly strange to us today, and it is hard to imagine a parishioner calling a priest to check out mildew in the bathroom.

The largest and most important set of laws within Leviticus, known as the Holiness Code, is found in chapters 17–26. This section was probably originally a separate work incorporated into the book of Leviticus in its final form. It takes its title from the often-repeated phrase, "You shall be holy, for I the LORD your God am holy" (Lev 19:2 et al.). It is also found in abbreviated forms, such as "I am the LORD your God" (e.g., Lev 18:2) and "I am the LORD" (e.g., Lev 18:5).

Holiness Code: a law code that is found in Lev 17–26. It takes its name from the repeated call, "Be holy, for I the LORD your God am holy."

This section covers a wide range of issues that resist easy classification. What they have in common is the fact that breaking any of these commands compromises the holiness of the people. In other words, each of the individual laws in the Holiness Code is merely an illustration of what it means to be holy. "Be holy" is the command; the particular laws are concrete examples of how to follow the command.

Although a full treatment of the Holiness Code is beyond the scope of this book, a look at the laws in Lev 19:1–22 provides a sample of the types of laws that are found here. The chapter opens with several short commands that parallel those in the Ten Commandments: honor your parents, keep the Sabbath, and do not make idols. These are followed by instructions concerning the eating of the offering of well-being. Then come laws dealing with the harvest, some of which must be left in the field for the feeding of the poor. Verses 11–13 return to laws similar to those in the Decalogue, while verses 14–16 deal with how to treat other people. The next two verses address hatred and revenge, ending with the well-known command to "love your neighbor as yourself." Immediately after this great command come more mundane prohibitions against crossbreeding animals, seeding a field with two different plants, and wearing clothing made from two different types of material. The last few verses deal with how a man is to treat a female slave with whom he has had sex. The rest of the chapter continues this seemingly random movement from one topic to another, touching on subjects ranging from fruit trees to divination to the practice of standing up when an elderly person entered a room.

Although the three sections in Lev 8–26 may seem quite distinct in terms of content, one unifying theme runs through each of them: holiness. You may recall from chapter 3 that it was necessary for the people to be holy so they could live safely with God in their midst. So the sanctification of the priests in Lev 8–10 is important, as the priests were the ones who had the closest approach to God. Chapters 11–16 maintain the holiness of the people by focusing on those aspects of everyday life that bring about impurity, while the Holiness Code in chapters 17–26 shows the people how to live holy lives. In each case, the issue at hand is maintaining the safety of the community and its ability to dwell with God. And when the people become impure, they have recourse to the sacrifices in Lev 1–7, which restore them to a state of holiness.

Back to the Question of Ritual, Civil, and Ethical Laws

Now that we've had a quick look at Leviticus, let's think again about how the law is used. Remember that some scholars deal with the law by dividing the statutes into ritual, civil, and ethical laws. We can ignore the first two according to this scheme, but we are still bound by the ethical laws.

Leviticus 19:1–22 can serve as a test case for this method. After all, these laws reflect statutes found in the Ten Commandments, the ultimate ethical code. Most people would describe Lev 19:1–3 as ethical. We might consider verse 4 ethical as well, although prohibitions against idols might be considered ritual since they involve worship. Verses 5–8 are clearly ritual, dealing with questions regarding the offering of well-being. Verses 9–11 are ethical. Many people might classify verse 12 as ethical, since it deals with swearing in the name of God. But because such oaths were generally taken during legal proceedings, it is probably better to classify this verse as civil.

Verses 13–14 return to the ethical realm, while verses 15–16a belong to the realm of civil matters. Verses 16b–18 are ethical, containing the law that Jesus called the second greatest commandment. Verse 19, on the other hand, is difficult to classify. Some scholars categorize it as ritual, the category it seems to fit the best. But it is hard to imagine how exactly this verse qualifies as ritual. It does not involve worship or the cleanliness of the worshiper but instead focuses on preventing the mixing of different categories of material. Verses 20–22 can be classified as ethical, although in the midst of this passage the focus shifts from the ethical problem of sexual relations to the ritual question of how to make atonement.

Table 2 shows the breakdown of Lev 19:1–22. A quick glance at the distribution of the laws shows that it is highly unlikely that the ancient Israelites classified these laws according to ritual, civil, and ethical matters. If they did, it is hard to understand how they could have scattered these categories throughout the chapter in a seemingly random way. The laws jump back and forth from ritual to ethical to civil without any transition between them. In addition, several laws defy classification. Verse 19 only barely fits into ritual law, mainly because it clearly doesn't belong to the other categories. And verses 20–22 must be broken across two different categories, as they switch from one classification to another in the middle of the passage. In other words, these were simply not the categories that the ancient Israelites had in mind when they wrote Leviticus. And if that is the case, then we should abandon attempts to force the laws into categories that are foreign to them.

TABLE 2

Ritual	Civil	Ethical
		vv. 1–3
v. 4(?)		v. 4(?)
vv. 5–8		
		vv. 9–11
	v. 12	
		v. 13–14
	vv. 15–16a	
		v. 16b–18
v. 19(?)		
vv. 20–22(?)		vv. 20–22(?)

Conversations with the Law in Leviticus

To use the laws of Leviticus in the modern church, we need to come up with a new model that allows us to view the laws in this book as the word of God. Here are some new ways of looking at Leviticus:

First, pay attention to the aspects of grace. Because Christians usually come to Old Testament laws through the lens of the New Testament in general and the Apostle Paul in particular, we tend to contrast law with grace. But that is not what the writers of Leviticus did. Leviticus is one of the most grace-filled books in the Bible. Its first seven chapters, discussed in the previous chapters, provide God's means of grace to the people for when they failed to follow the law. Far from being a burden that the people had to bear, the law was, for them, a means of freedom.

Second, use the categories proposed by Leviticus. Leave behind extraneous categories such as "civil," "ritual," and "ethical." We must read Leviticus on its own terms and let it provide its own categories. And Leviticus very clearly gives us such a category in the idea of holiness, the concept that binds the independent parts of the book into a whole. All laws in Leviticus, regardless of their content, were meant to teach the Israelites how to live holy lives. They didn't follow these laws to be saved—they had already been saved as a community in the exodus from Egypt. Instead, the statutes in Leviticus told the Israelites how to be holy so they could live safely with a holy God in their midst.

Holiness is a category that is greatly misunderstood today. We tend to think either of the holiness of objects (the host at the Eucharist, the altar dressings, and so on) or of people who have reached a certain level of ethical purity. While both of these definitions tell part of the story, they don't provide a full account of what it means to be holy. Holiness is simply a state of being in which all things that keep us apart from God have been removed. Unholy things defy easy categorization, as many things can be holy in one instance and not in the next. Our jobs, for instance, when approached through the idea of holiness, provide us with a way to serve others. When they cease functioning in that way and instead become a means of oppressing people or simply a way to enrich ourselves, they have become unholy elements that keep us from

God. Or our jobs can begin to consume us, taking up such a large part of our lives that they leave little room for God and our neighbor. When that happens, they have become unholy things in our midst, and they prevent us from being in full relationship with God. Anything, from a sin to a virtue, can become unholy when it keeps us from God.

Third, recognize that Leviticus calls us to examine ourselves for those things that keep us from God. This doesn't mean that we should apply Leviticus in a flat-footed way, simply following the laws blindly. Instead, we need to read Leviticus to understand the patterns of living it provides. For example, consider the laws on the treatment of the poor. Laws such as Lev 19:9–10 call for us not to

> *Leviticus calls us to examine ourselves for those things that keep us from God.*

try to press every bit of profit out of our business. Instead, we should allow the excess of our work overflow to provide for the poor. Similar laws are in Lev 19:13, which stipulates that the wages of workers are not to be held back overnight, because the poor live each day on what they have earned that day—so to deny them their pay is to deny them their lives. While not all such laws are to be applied literally, when they are read together, a pattern of living begins to emerge that can serve as a critique of our prevailing economic models. Leviticus, rich in such resources, can help us begin to imagine a more just culture, in which the benefits of goods and services are available to all people, including the poor. Leviticus, acting as a mirror, can show us those places in our lives where our actions, both individual and corporate, don't mesh with the call to be holy as God is holy.

Fourth, recognize the role of canon. When the early Jewish community, and later the early church, canonized the Bible, they didn't differentiate between different books of the Bible. To paraphrase George Orwell's dictum in *Animal Farm*, it is not the case that all Scriptures are the word of God but that some are more the word of God than others. In other words, Leviticus is just as important as the narratives in Genesis or the epistles of Paul. The canon, as a theological construct, calls us to read the Bible as a whole. Such an approach balances our understanding and allows all portions of the Bible to have their say. It pre-

> **Canonization:** the process of determining which books should be considered Scripture. A canon is a list of such books.

vents us from forming our own canon within a canon, reading special books repeatedly while ignoring others.

This canonical balance is especially important, ironically, for the books that we understand the least. Because Leviticus seems to be a confusing and irrelevant book, we have a tendency to leave it aside in favor of books of the Bible that we do understand. But it is worth noting that no one ever came to an understanding of a book by not reading it. It is precisely because this book is difficult that we need to return to it time and time again, wrestling with it and refusing to let it go until it provides us with a blessing.[4] And as we come to understand those books that were unfamiliar to us, we will come to a better understanding of those books that we thought we already knew. Only as a whole is the Bible a sufficient witness to God's actions, and when we don't treat it as a whole, we skew our perspective of God.

Finally, in reading Leviticus, we need to acknowledge the continuity of the covenants. The Bible describes God's covenant with the ancient Israelites in the Old Testament while treating his covenant with the whole world in the New Testament. Because of this division between the two, and in part because of the words "Old" and "New" that modify the Testaments, we often think of the covenant with the Jews as a covenant that has been superseded by the new covenant of Jesus Christ. But although there are differences between the two, it is a difference of degree and not of substance. Both covenants depend on grace, and both offer salvation through faith. The main difference is that the first covenant was only with Israel, while the second is with the whole world. Yet the first covenant always looked to the wider world, while the second constantly acknowledges its debt to and continuity with the people of Israel. In fact, the second is best understood as simply an expansion of the first. As Paul puts it, we have been grafted into the same tree of which Israel is a part (Rom 11:17–24).

This continuity has implications for our reading of the laws in Leviticus. If our covenant is similar to the covenant to which Leviticus testifies, then it can still serve as the word of God for us. Far from being a book that has become irrelevant or has been superseded, Leviticus still provides us with patterns of living that show us what it means to live as the people of God. Although our circumstances in the twenty-first century may require an adaptation of the laws to a new situation, the God who gave these laws is the same God who has called us into relationship in Christ Jesus. The call of Leviticus to be holy as God is holy (Lev 19:2) is echoed in Jesus' call for us to be perfect as God is perfect (Matt 5:48).

Holiness for the Church

Though there may be many ways to look at the book of Leviticus through the lens of our Christian faith, it will never be an easy book for the church, and it is not likely to enjoy a surge of popularity among Christians anytime soon. Its world is too far removed from ours for us to ever be entirely comfortable with it. But perhaps that is a good thing. It is far too easy to become so at home with the Bible that it never challenges us. But if that happens, the book of Leviticus will always be there, calling us into a different world and suggesting new options for serving God and loving our neighbors. As we continually wrestle with Leviticus and explore how it can be the word of God for us, we may be motivated to reassess our relationship with the more comfortable books of the Bible. If we are open to allowing Leviticus to shape our understanding of life in God, we may come to a richer understanding of the entire Bible. When that happens, we may begin to read the Scriptures through the lens of holiness, seeking to determine how we can be holy as the Lord our God is holy.

CHAPTER FIVE

The Law in Numbers

The church may have neglected the book of Leviticus, long on laws and short on narrative, but not so the book of Numbers, which is packed with well-known stories. Among these is the famous tale of the Israelite spies sent into Canaan who bring back a report of "a land that flows with milk and honey" (Num 14:8). Numbers is also home to the stories of Balaam and his talking donkey (chs. 22–24), Aaron's budding rod (17:1–11), and the bronze serpent (21:4–9). Over the years, the narratives in Numbers have provided fodder for many sermons and theological discussion within the church. But still, Christians haven't paid any more attention to the legal sections in Numbers than they have to the laws in the rest of the Pentateuch.

The book of Numbers presents the reader with a rich variety of material, from census lists to legal formulations to itineraries to historical reports. And just as the genres in Numbers present little uniformity, so does the legal material. The laws in Numbers bounce around from those governing priests to those affecting women to those concerning Nazirites. And unlike Leviticus, where the laws can be broken down into sections with consistent themes, the laws in Numbers are scattered throughout the book. There is little discernable reasoning for why particular laws are grouped together, and no large body of laws can be discerned. Laws alternate with narrative in a seemingly random way. Such a lack of order has sometimes caused scholars to label Numbers the dumping grounds of the Pentateuch. It sometimes appears that Numbers simply became the home for any material that the authors couldn't put into any other book of the Torah.

By the Numbers

The English name of the book of Numbers derives from the two census accounts found in chapters 1 and 26. One census was taken while the people were at Mount Sinai, and the other was taken at the end of the forty years of wandering in the wilderness, when all of the first generation had died. Although these census reports provide a minimal framework for the book, the Hebrew title *b^emidbar* ("in the desert"), taken from a word in the first verse of the book, better describes its overall setting.

The story in Numbers moves the people from Mount Sinai to the edge of the Promised Land. In the first ten chapters, the people are still at the mountain of God, where they have been since Exodus 19. Within these ten chapters are the first census report, an account of the duties of the Levites, and the celebration of the second Passover, after the original Passover in Egypt. Having been at Sinai for almost a year, the people set out at the command of God in Num 10:11. This second section of the book, which runs through Num 20:14, contains the account of the spies who were sent into Canaan and the punishment of the Israelites for doubting that God could give them victory over the Canaanites. Their punishment—the forty years of wandering in the wilderness—is related in this section as well. Also found here are numerous complaint stories and rebellions, culminating in Moses' disobedience at Meribah (Num 20:1–13), which kept him from ever entering the Promised Land.

The third section of the book runs from 20:15 through 31:54. It covers the new generation that would actually enter Canaan after the forty years of wandering. This section provides an account of their journey from the wilderness of Sinai around the eastern side of the Dead Sea. They passed the kingdoms of Edom and Moab along the way, entering into battle with Moab and other Amorite kings. These battles formed the first stage of the conquest that is primarily recounted in the book of Joshua. The book concludes in 32:1–36:13 with a description of preparations for further conquests. The end of Numbers leaves the Israelites on the Plains of Moab, at the northeast corner of the Dead Sea.

The Law in Numbers

Interspersed within these narratives are the legal sections of Numbers. A large chunk of this material is found in the first ten chapters, and this constitutes the largest block of laws in the book. These laws are hardly homogeneous, however, and they have been woven together with a census account, a passage listing the offerings brought by the heads of each of the tribes, and a report of the consecration of the Levites. Other legal texts are scattered much more widely. For example, a passage detailing the portions of the offerings reserved for the priests and Levites has been coupled with the instructions for preparing the ashes of a red heifer, which would cleanse those who had come into contact with a corpse (Num 18–19). These two passages in turn have been inserted between the report of Aaron's budding rod (ch. 17) and the Israelites' murmurings at Meribah (ch. 20). Other sections of laws occur in Num 15:1–31, which gives the rules for offerings; Num 28–29, which stipulate which sacrifices must be made at which festivals and holy days; and Num 30:1–16, which gives laws concerning vows made by women.

Because of the variety of laws found in Numbers and their wide dispersal within the text, approaching the laws in order is not particularly helpful. The subject of the laws changes so frequently that such an approach can be confusing. A better strategy is to divide the laws according to their subject matter. Although such a systemization of the laws still leaves a sizable category that can only be labeled "miscellaneous," the majority of the laws can be grouped in this way. The largest of these groups consists of laws concerning priests and Levites, laws regulating sacrifices and offerings, and laws regarding women. We looked at sacrificial laws already in chapter 3, but each of the other two categories, along with a few miscellaneous laws, will be considered here in turn.

LAWS CONCERNING PRIESTS AND LEVITES

The title of the book of Leviticus derives from the fact that a great deal of its material deals with the priests, who were descendants of Levi. But priestly Levites comprised only a minority of the Levites, and in the terminology of Numbers, the priests are not called Levites at all. The word *Levites* in Numbers refers to the rest of the descendants of Levi, those who were not allowed to serve as priests. They were given special tasks with regard to the tabernacle and as assistants to the priests. Because these laws governing the Levites are found only in the book of Numbers, "Leviticus" would be a more appropriate title for the fourth book of the Pentateuch than for the third.

The Levites were divided into three clans, each of which was named after one of the three sons of Levi: Gershon, Kohath, and Merari (Gen 46:11). Chapter 4 of Numbers provides a detailed account of their tasks in relation to the tabernacle. The Kohathites, discussed in Num 4:1–20, were given charge over the ritual objects used in worship that resided in the tabernacle, including the ark of the covenant. They were to transport these objects whenever the Israelites broke camp to move to another location, but they were not allowed to see them. They had to wait until the Aaronic priests had covered each of the pieces with coverings of leather and cloth, and only then could they approach the objects. It is interesting to note that the Kohathites had charge over these most sacred objects even though Kohath was the second-born son of Levi. Their elevated position might have been due to the fact that Kohath was the grandfather of both Moses and Aaron (Exod 6:18–20).

Aaronic: pertaining to the main priestly line in Israel, which was descended from Moses' brother, Aaron.

The other two Levitical clans were the Gershonites and the Merarites, the descendants of the first- and third-born sons of Levi, whose responsibilities are laid out in Num 4:21–33. The Gershonites were to carry the curtains of the tabernacle, while the Merarites were to have charge of the poles and stands that formed the framework of the tent. Like the Kohathites, the Gershonites and Merarites were not allowed to view the holy objects in the tabernacle but were to wait until the priests had covered them before taking down the tent. The marching order for each of the three Levitical clans is given in Num 10:17–21. The Gershonites and the Merarites were to march well ahead of the Kohathites so they could have the tent set up by the time the Kohathites arrived with the sacred objects.

As we learned in chapter 2, twelve tribes of Israel camped around the tabernacle in the wilderness period, with three tribes situated on each side. The Levites weren't included in this number, so the two half tribes of Ephraim and Manasseh were separated to bring the number back up to twelve. According to Num 3:14–39, another part of the Levites' duties was to serve as a buffer zone between the tribes of Israel and the tabernacle. Although the tabernacle at the center of the encampment symbolized God's place at the center of their communal life, the holiness of the tabernacle was a danger to the people. Any encroach-

The tabernacle at the center of the encampment symbolized God's place at the center of communal life.

ment on this holiness could bring disaster on the people. To avert such disasters, the Levites were supposed to camp around the tabernacle, with each of the clans forming a barrier on one side. The Kohathites were to camp to the south of the tent, with the Gershonites and Merarites to the west and north, respectively. The sons of Aaron and Moses, the priests, were to camp on the east side, where the entrance to the tent was located.

In addition to their physical service at the tabernacle, the Levites served another function within Israel. According to the Israelites' theology, when the first child to be born to a woman was a male, that child belonged to God (Exod 13:11–16). The same rule applied to animals as well (Lev 27:26–27; Deut 15:19–23). The reason for this was that God had brought the Israelites out of Egypt through the killing of the firstborn Egyptian males during the Passover, and in return the firstborn male Israelites belonged to God. For an animal, belonging to God meant it had to be sacrificed, except in the case of unclean or blemished animals, which were redeemed with an appropriate payment to the temple. Obviously, though, human children were not to be sacrificed. This required a substitution to be put forward for the human children, and the Levites served as this substitution. God accepted their service at the tent of meeting in place of the death of the firstborn Israelites (Num 3:11–13, 40–51). If the number of firstborn males in Israel surpassed the number of Levites, those children could be redeemed at a price of five shekels of silver (approximately two ounces), paid to the priests (Num 18:16).

LAWS CONCERNING WOMEN

Several laws in Numbers deal primarily with women, such as the law regarding women's vows found in Numbers 30:1–16. The main laws concerning women can be divided into two different groups. The first group, consisting of laws governing women who were suspected of adultery, is found in Num 5:11–31. The passage deals with a woman who hadn't been caught in the act of adultery but whose husband suspected her of having been unfaithful. The determining factor for invoking this law wasn't the woman's actions but her husband's suspicions, referred to as a "spirit of jealousy." In such a case, this law required a rite that determined the woman's innocence or guilt. The woman was to hold a grain offering meant to bring to mind her sins. She then took an oath of innocence, after which she drank holy water mixed with dust from the tabernacle floor. If she was guilty, her "uterus [would] drop" and her "womb [would] discharge," phrases that are found only here in the Old Testament. The precise meaning is unclear but probably refers either to a miscarriage if the woman is pregnant or to future infertility. If the woman was found to be innocent, she was cleared of all charges and nothing happened. Such trials by ordeal were known in other ancient Near Eastern laws as well.

For modern readers, several thoughts immediately come to mind. Why was only the woman made to undergo the ordeal? What about her suspected partner? And why did the woman's husband have a right to publicly humiliate her this way just because he was suspicious? These are, of course, valid questions with no easy explanation. But it is important to note that, unlike in some societies, the woman was not automatically considered guilty. The husband did not have the right to immediately bring an accusation against her that could easily lead to her death (cf. Deut 22:22–24). Instead, the woman had to undergo the trial to determine her status.

In addition, the importance of the law in ancient Israel probably had little to do with the husband's rights. The passage clearly states that the issue is whether the wife had defiled herself (Num 5:13, 20). If she had, then she was a danger to the community, since impurity in the midst of Israel placed the people in danger of coming into contact with the holiness of God and thereby being destroyed. This rite was more about determining whether the woman needed to be cleansed from sin than about sanctioning the husband's rights.

The second category of laws concerning women centers around the daughters of a man named Zelophehad, found in Num 27:1–11 and 36:1–13. In the first passage, we read that the five daughters came to Moses because their father had died, leaving no sons. Under such conditions, we would expect the inheritance to pass to the nearest male relative, usually a brother. The daughters, however, were concerned that this would keep their father's name from being passed on to future generations. They petitioned Moses to allow them to inherit their father's portion of the property. Moses asked God about this case, and God instituted a law for future generations stating that women could in fact inherit in cases in which a father died with no male heirs.

The story of Zelophehad's daughters continues in Num 36:1–13. Other members of their tribe were concerned that the daughters might marry members of other tribes, thereby transferring their property to another tribe. Tribal inheritance was supposed to remain within the tribe, and the marriage of the daughter into another clan would have broken this law. Moses agreed and issued a command that the women had to marry within their own tribe, thereby preserving the integrity of the inheritance.

Such a law may sound restrictive to modern ears, but it would have been less so to the initial readers. In our modern society, marriages between people of different social classes, states, or even countries are not uncommon. However, in ancient Israel, as in many societies organized on tribal grounds, marriages outside the immediate group were much more infrequent. Marriage to those who were very distantly related or not related at all was discouraged, as was marriage to immediate family. The ideal was marriage to someone who was related but not too closely. This allowed property to remain within the immediate clan, or at least within the tribe. Notice, for example, that Abraham married his half sister (Gen 20:12), while both Isaac and Jacob married their cousins (Gen 24, 29). This command to marry within the tribe, while theoretically reducing the eligible candidates for women to marry, was probably not a major factor for most women.

LAWS CONCERNING NAZIRITES

A number of laws that don't fit into the two categories discussed above are also found in Numbers. Among these are laws concerning unclean persons (Num 5:1–4), a command to make trumpets to regulate the march of the Israelite camp (10:1–10), a law requiring a blue thread to be worn in the fringe of garments (15:37–41), and a section laying out the boundaries of the Holy Land (34:1–29). Among the more interesting of the miscellaneous laws, however, are those covering the Nazirite. This text is found in Num 6:1–21.

The word *Nazirite* comes from the Hebrew verb *nazar*, which means "to consecrate" or "to separate." A Nazirite is one who had separated himself or herself and therefore obtained a higher level of holiness. The precise object of the separation is unclear. Nazirites may have been considered separate from the rest of the people, or they may have been seen as set apart for a particular task. The verb *separate* may also refer to the fact that they were set apart from anything that would have defiled them. According to some texts, a person could be a Nazirite for life, such as Samson and Samuel, both of whom were set apart as Nazirites from their births (Judg 13:5; 1 Sam 1:11). The book of Numbers, however, doesn't mention such lifelong Nazirites. Instead, it focuses on those who took a vow to be a Nazirite for a limited period of time.

The laws governing the Nazirite are fairly straightforward, even though the precise purpose of each rule isn't always clear. Nazirites had to follow three requirements. A Nazirite was not allowed to cut his or her hair during the period of the vow. This passage exhibits a repeated emphasis on the sacredness of the Nazirite's head, singling it out as the focus of their consecration. Only when their vows were completed were they allowed to shave their heads, and this had to be done in a ceremony at the tabernacle. Their hair was then burned on the altar, along with the sacrifices they made at the completion of their vows. Nazirites also were prohibited from eating grapes or any products made from grapes, including wine and vinegar.

The third requirement for the Nazirite was that he or she not come into contact with a dead body. So strict was this requirement that a Nazirite couldn't violate this rule even if a member of his or her immediate family died. The only other person among the Israelites who followed this injunction was the high priest (Lev 21:11), a fact that highlights the holiness of the Nazirite vow. Nazirites who did accidentally come into contact with a dead body had to purify themselves for seven days, including shaving their heads. This is in contrast to the law for a non-Nazirite, who could be purified by being sprinkled with water mixed with the ashes of a red heifer (Numbers 19). After being purified, the Nazirite would have to begin the time of consecration again, as the time up until that point would not count toward the fulfillment of the Nazirite's vow.

Even though the laws that a Nazirite had to follow are clear, the purpose for taking such a vow isn't. Nowhere does the Old Testament give the reason for the Nazirite vow, although many scholars suggest it was to carry out a particular task. The only evidence backing this suggestion comes from the lives of Samson and Samuel, both of whom were Nazirites. Both were considered judges, although Samson fulfilled this role more precisely than Samuel, who was also considered to be a prophet and a priest. Although Samuel's status as a Nazirite isn't mentioned again after his birth, the Nazirite vow plays a major role in the story of Samson. While most people are familiar with the story of Samson losing his strength when his hair was cut, note that earlier in the story Samson had violated the other two laws governing Nazirites. In Judg 14:5–9, we read that Samson ate honey out of a lion that he had killed, thereby violating the prohibition against contact with a corpse. And although it is not explicitly stated, Samson likely drank wine at his wedding feast (Judg 14:10–20). Notice also that the lion he killed was in a vineyard (Judg 14:5), further suggesting the connection with grape products. By the time we read of Samson getting his hair cut in Judges 16, therefore, Samson had already violated two out of three of the rules. The cutting of his hair was merely the final act in his downward slide.[1] Since Samson's ability to carry out his job as a judge was directly related to his Nazirite status, this lends credence to the idea that a Nazirite vow was undertaken to maintain holiness in connection with a particular task. This would also match the short-term nature of the Nazirite vow as depicted in Numbers.

Conversations with the Law in Numbers

The legal material in the book of Numbers presents the reader with a wide variety of subjects covering many varied areas of life. Such diversity automatically calls for equally diverse reflection on how these laws can be appropriated for the life of the church today. The underexplored territory of Numbers provides a wealth of material for the theological imagination. The following discussion is intended not to be exhaustive but to suggest some ways that the legal material could be used.

At first glance, the office that Levites would seem to parallel most closely is the office of deacon in the modern church. After all, the word *deacon* is derived from a Greek word meaning "servant," and that is precisely the role the Levites played. And within the worship service, deacons have the responsibility of setting the table prior to the celebration of the Eucharist by the priest, which is similar to the responsibilities that the Levites had with respect to the ritual objects used in worship. And, like Levites, deacons are not to perform priestly service. Deacons, of course, have the responsibility of serving the community outside the worship service as well, so their roles are not precisely parallel with those of the Levites, but the similarities between these two offices suggest that reflection on the work of the various Levitical clans would be profitable for deacons.

To limit the Levitical laws to deacons, however, would suppress much of the richness of this material, especially since the deacons aren't the only ones who assist the priest during worship. Within the churches of the Anglican Communion, a number of other altar servants are common: acolytes, chalicists, crucifers, thurifers, torch bearers, and altar guilds. Each of these plays a role similar to that of the Levites. The crucifer, for instance, carries the cross, the symbol of

Christ's presence in the Eucharist, much as the Kohathites carried the ark of the covenant, the symbol of God's presence in the tabernacle. The Kohathites also carried the candelabra that illuminated the tabernacle, just as the torch bearers accompany the crucifer into the service. And, like the Levites, altar guilds are responsible for the care of the holy vessels between services. The parallel

The crucifer carries the cross, the symbol of Christ's presence in the Eucharist, much as the Kohathites carried the ark of the covenant, the symbol of God's presence in the tabernacle.

between those roles should suggest to us the holiness of these jobs. The material in Numbers shows that, far from being jobs that can be given to anyone willing to do them, they are jobs that require a sense of holiness and reverence in service. The passages in Numbers that deal with Levites could be used quite profitably in the training of acolytes and other servants at the altar. The incorporation of such Bible study into the training of acolytes would move the training from merely covering the practical issues of where to stand and when to bow. It would bring the theological and spiritual meaning of these offices to the fore.

The laws concerning the Nazirites seem to present an area ripe with theological possibilities. Recent years have seen an increase in interest in spiritual formation and a focus on traditional spiritual disciplines. Within such a context, it is not hard to imagine how the concept of a nazirite vow could be adapted to modern practice. Such a vow would allow a person to adopt a particular rule of life (to use the traditional monastic terminology) for a short period of time, during which the person would follow set guidelines for spiritual practices. In keeping with the idea of the Nazirite vow, such a vow could be undertaken as a way of preparing for or carrying out a particular task. It also could be used in preparation for major life changes, such as the period leading up to a marriage or a new job. The Nazirite vow could even be used as a method of repentance, either for specific sins or for a period of self-examination such as Lent. In this connection, it is interesting to note that some Christians in the early church, including the Apostle Paul, continued the practice of the Nazirite vow (Acts 18:18; 21:17–26).

To maintain the spirit of the Nazirite laws, however, such a practice must not be merely a private vow taken by an individual. Instead, the initial vow should be taken within the context of a worship service, making the vow a public statement of devotion and allowing the congregation to support the Nazirite during the vow's duration. The completion of the period of dedication should likewise come to a close in a liturgical setting, with thanks given to God both by the individual for God's help and by the congregation in recognition of God's call to holiness. As in the laws of Numbers 6, some outward and visible sign should accompany the vow. Although the shaving of one's head might be outside the bounds of practicality in modern society, some other equally visible sign could be used. One suggestion would be a special cross that could be blessed during the initial worship service and worn by the devotee during the time of the vow, only to be returned to the congregation upon the vow's completion.

Summing Up Numbers

In between the well-known stories of the book of Numbers lies a great deal of legal materials that can enrich the life and worship of the church. Laws covering a wide variety of subjects call our attention to the important work performed not only by the select few of the priesthood but by all those who serve. And while Numbers acknowledges the holiness of those who are called to lifelong service, it also recognizes that not everyone can make such vows. The institution of the Nazirites provides a way for people to pledge themselves to God for short periods of time for special tasks. The special state of holiness is not reserved for the priests but may be obtained by any whom God has called. Numbers asks—and perhaps even demands—that those of us in the modern church recognize God's call to each of us to serve in holiness. Although recognizing a difference in role, Numbers does not distinguish between the holiness of priests and that of laity. All are God's servants, whether they serve in the world, at the altar, or both.

Numbers asks—and perhaps even demands—that those of us in the modern church recognize God's call to each of us to serve in holiness.

 The Law in Deuteronomy

At the end of the book of Numbers, the people of Israel reach the end of a journey that began long ago and far away in Egypt. They were formed into a covenant community by an act of God at Mount Sinai, and after traveling through the desert for forty years, they now stand at the edge of the Promised Land. They have reached the northeast corner of the Dead Sea and are ready to enter into the land flowing with milk and honey, so close they can almost taste it. At this point, however, Moses decides to deliver an extended sermon rehearsing the history of Israel and restating the law. This sermon comprises the book of Deuteronomy—and delays the entry into Canaan by thirty-four chapters.

Moving into Deuteronomy

Entering the book of Deuteronomy after having read the laws in Exodus, Leviticus, and Numbers means leaving behind one world and entering another. As we saw in the introduction, the first four books of the Pentateuch derive from one set of sources—known as the Yahwistic (J) and Priestly (P) sources—while Deuteronomy derives from

D: the letter used in source criticism to designate the book of Deuteronomy.

another source known as D. And while the material in J and P seems to have originated in official circles in Jerusalem, Deuteronomy comes to the scene as an outsider. Although the book sets itself up as a retelling of the law—the name *Deuteronomy* means "second law"—the actual content of the law in Deuteronomy is sometimes strikingly different from that found in the books of Exodus through Numbers.

Although the origin of the traditions in the book of Deuteronomy isn't clear, the Bible does contain a record of the first time the book of Deuteronomy made an appearance in history. In 2 Kgs 22, King Josiah of Judah (ruled 639–609 BCE) restores the temple in Jerusalem. During the restoration, the high priest Hilkiah reports that a book of the law has been found in the temple. The book is read before Josiah, who tears his clothes when he realizes that he and the people of Judah haven't been following this law. He then undertakes a reform of Israelite religion to bring it into line with the regulations found in the newly discovered book.

The name Deuteronomy *means "second law"—the actual content of the law in Deuteronomy is sometimes strikingly different from that found in the books of Exodus through Numbers.*

Because of the nature of these reforms, most scholars think the book found in the temple contained the core of Deuteronomy as we now have it. For instance, Josiah removed the idols to Baal and Asherah from the temple in Jerusalem (2 Kgs 23:4), which parallels the concern with these gods found in Deut 13:6–11. He also destroyed the high places, the standing stones, and the Asherah poles (2 Kgs 23:13–14) as commanded in Deut 12:2–4. And he put an end to male prostitution as part of the worship of Yahweh (2 Kgs 23:7 // Deut 23:17–18). Because of these parallels, the book found in the temple seems to have included at least Deut 12–26 and also may have contained chapters 5–11. Chapters 1–4, along with 27–30 and 31–34, were added at a later time.

Some scholars have suggested that the book of Deuteronomy was written by a reform-minded group at the end of the seventh century BCE. This group, which may have included some of the priests in Jerusalem, placed the book in the temple, where it would be found and taken to King Josiah. But regardless of when the book itself was written, it is clear that the traditions in Deuteronomy precede the seventh century BCE. At the end of the eighth century BCE, for instance, King Hezekiah (ruled 727–698 BCE), the great-grandfather of Josiah, undertook a reform that also seems to have been Deuteronomistic in character (2 Kings 18). It is impossible to say when the laws in Deuteronomy originated, but they were at least circulating in some form by the eighth century before Christ.

Yet despite the fact that the laws of Deuteronomy arose alongside those found in Exodus through Numbers, it is likely they were a minority opinion accepted by few within the official religious establishment in Jerusalem. The books of 1 and 2 Kings, which record the reigns of the kings of Israel and Judah, rate each king on whether or not he followed the laws in Deuteronomy. In Israel, none of the kings is listed as adhering to the regulations in Deuteronomy. Among the rulers in Judah, only Hezekiah and Josiah followed these laws completely, while others followed them either in part or not at all. In fact, the books of 1 and 2 Kings attribute the destruction of Israel to the people's failure to follow Deuteronomy (2 Kgs 17:7–18). Only during the exile and the period immediately afterward did Deuteronomy become accepted by the majority. When the canon of the Torah was drawn up in the late fifth century, therefore, Deuteronomy found itself placed on equal footing with the other books of the Pentateuch.

Overview of the Laws

In the final form of the book of Deuteronomy, the laws in chapters 12–26 are framed by several opening and closing sections. Preceding the laws are two sets of sermons delivered by Moses. The first, in 1:1–4:43, recounts the history of Israel from the time the people left Mount Horeb—Deuteronomy's name for Sinai—through their wanderings in the wilderness, up to the point when they reached the edge of the Promised Land. This is followed by a second sermon in 4:44–11:32, which exhorts the people to follow the law. Following the laws in chapters 12–26, chapters 27–30 contain a series of blessings and curses. The blessings would come if the law was followed, while the curses would accompany disobedience. Moses commands these blessings and curses to be read on Mount Ebal when the people had found rest in the land of Canaan (Deut 27:1–8), a command carried out by Joshua at the end of the conquest (Josh 8:30–35). This is followed by the last words of Moses in chapters 31–33 and the death of Moses in chapter 34.

Although this introduction describes Deuteronomy as a minority opinion within preexilic Judah, many of the laws in Deuteronomy are in fact similar to those in Exodus through Numbers, even if they are given slightly different emphases. For example, the kosher laws in Deut 14:3–21 proscribe many of the same foods as Lev 11:1–47. Deuteronomy 16:1–17 covers many of the festivals found in other parts of the Pentateuch, such as the Sabbath, the Feast of Weeks, and the Festival of Booths. The requirement in Deut 26:1–11 that the firstfruits of the harvest be brought to the temple is parallel with Exod 23:19; Lev 23:10; and Num 15:20–21. And, of course, Deut 5:1–21 contains a version of the Ten Commandments almost identical to the one in Exod 20:1–17. There are many more examples of similarities, but these are enough to show that while Deuteronomy may have been a minority opinion, it didn't promote an entirely different vision of the law of Moses.

The question of the order of the laws in Deut 12–26 doesn't have an easy answer. At first reading, the laws don't seem to follow a logical sequence. The topics jump from worship in chapters 12–13 to kosher laws in chapter 14 to festivals in chapters 15–16. Some scholars, however, have suggested that there is a deeper level of structure to the text that explains why the laws are ordered as they are. They have proposed that the laws in chapters 12–26 are arranged to reflect the arrangement of the Ten Commandments.[1] Look at the correspondence between the Decalogue and the law in Deuteronomy in the following chart:[2]

Deut 12–13	First, second, and third commandments
Deut 14:28–16:17	Fourth commandment
Deut 16:18–18:22	Fifth commandment
Deut 19:1–21:9	Sixth commandment begins and ends the section, with the eighth, tenth, and ninth commandments in between
Deut 22:13–30	Seventh commandment
Deut 23–26	Eighth and tenth commandments

While the correlations are suggestive, they are not altogether convincing. For one thing, the commandments don't fall in the same order in Deuteronomy 12–26 as they do in the Decalogue. The sixth commandment is interrupted by commandments eight, ten, and nine (in that order). The eighth and tenth commandments are also repeated at the end, without the ninth commandment.

There are other difficulties too. While it is easy to accept that the first three commandments are reflected in the laws requiring worship only of Yahweh and the exclusion of foreign practices in Deut 12–13, not all of the laws match up this neatly. Is the fifth commandment to honor parents really expanded to cover respect for all authority? If so, why is the authority of the king so limited in Deut 17:14–20? And how can this scheme account for the sections in Deut 21:22–22:12 and 24:6–25:4 where the laws appear to follow no order whatsoever? Given these problems, the theory that the Ten Commandments are the structural principle behind Deut 12–26 must remain merely suggestive, and the idea that the laws are ordered randomly or according to some principle yet to be discovered must be kept in mind.

CITIES OF REFUGE

Because a number of the laws in Deuteronomy are paralleled in other books of the Pentateuch, it is not necessary to repeat the discussion of those laws here. One set of laws found in both Numbers and Deuteronomy has not yet been discussed, however. These are the laws in Num 35:9–28 and Deut 19:1–13 describing the cities of refuge in ancient Israel. According to these passages, the Israelites were supposed to set up cities to serve as places of sanctuary for those guilty of certain crimes. Numbers 35:13 states that six cities were to be chosen. Moses set up three of these cities east of the Jordan (Deut 4:41–43) before his death. Deuteronomy 19:2 calls for three cities to the west of the Jordan, but because these cities could be designated as places of sanctuary only after the people of Israel had taken control of Canaan, this command wasn't carried out until Josh 20:1–9. Deuteronomy also makes provision for additional cities if Israel became large enough to need them (Deut 19:8–10). The six cities were chosen from among the Levitical cities, so they didn't belong to the eleven tribes given land in Canaan. The purpose of the cities was to protect people who committed unintentional manslaughter.

According to the Mosaic law, anyone who killed another person was to be put to death. The reason for this was that the ground was polluted by blood that had been shed, and only the shedding of the killer's blood would make atonement (Gen 9:5–6). This understanding of the pollution of the ground is found as early as Gen 4:10, where Abel's blood is said to cry out to God from the ground. The task of vengeance fell to the nearest male relative of the person who had been killed. This relative had the right to take the life of the killer, thereby atoning for the murder.

The cities of refuge came about because of situations when the killing of the killer would bring about further injustice. Such was the situation when the killing was unintentional. Numbers 35 and Deuteronomy 19 describe several cases that amount to unintentional manslaughter. Such cases include accidents and, apparently, unpremeditated crimes of passion. Although the pollution of the ground required that the killer be put to death, the law recognized that in these cases the person didn't deserve death. The Torah therefore set aside six cities to which a person who committed unintentional manslaughter could flee.

The cities were spread throughout the territory of Israel so that no one would have to go too far to reach one. If the killer could make it to one of these cities, he would be safe. If the avenger caught up with the killer before he or she entered a city of refuge, vengeance could be taken without incurring bloodguilt. In such cases, no further action needed to be taken. If the killer managed to make it safely to a city of refuge, a trial would be held to determine if the killing was in fact unintentional. If the killer was found to be an enemy of the victim, it was assumed that the killing was premeditated and the killer would be handed over to the avenger to be put to death.

In cases in which the killing was ruled to be accidental, the killer was required to live in the city of refuge until the death of the current high priest. The idea behind this limitation may have been that the death of the high priest atoned for the shed blood. After the priest died, the accused was free to return home and was not to be killed by the avenger. But if the killer left the city while the high priest was still alive, he or she could be put to death by the avenger if caught outside the city walls. While the concept may seem strange to a modern understanding of justice, the cities of refuge provided a balance between competing claims of justice—between the blood of the victim and the innocence of the unintentional killer.

Laws Unique to Deuteronomy

As we have seen, Deuteronomy contains a number of laws not found in other books of the Pentateuch. Among these are laws concerning kings and prophets, as well as laws governing holy wars. Deuteronomy also lays out special regulations for worship that are quite different in character from their counterparts in Exodus through Numbers. Each of these special laws will be examined in turn, with an eye toward understanding the unique perspective they bring to this final book of the law.

WORSHIP

Laws concerning worship in ancient Israel are by no means unique to Deuteronomy. Exodus, Leviticus, and Numbers all contain laws that detailed when worship was to occur, how it was to be carried out, and who was allowed to participate. What's different about the laws in Deuteronomy is not the subject but the way the subject is addressed. In this book, the focus is less on the mechanics of sacrifice and the correct times for festivals and more on which practices and locations are unacceptable for the worship of Yahweh. The primary text that deals with these questions is found in Deuteronomy 12.

In Deuteronomy the focus is less on the mechanics of sacrifice and the correct times for festivals and more on which practices and locations are unacceptable for the worship of Yahweh.

The first question—acceptable worship practices—is an important one for Deuteronomy. Several objects were forbidden within the Israelite ritual. In the NRSV, the three main items are called pillars, sacred poles, and idols (Deut 12:3). While Deuteronomy presents these objects as Canaanite paraphernalia adopted by the Israelites, in reality they were probably well-established objects within the Israelite religion that Deuteronomy, as a document aimed at reform, was seeking to remove. Although the prohibition against idols is well-known within the Bible, the other two objects require some explanation.

The first object, the pillar, is known from archaeological excavations. It was a stone, usually undecorated, set up to serve as a place where the deity could manifest itself. The best evidence for the use of such a standing stone—as it is often called in translation—is found in Gen 28:10–22. In the well-known passage of Jacob's dream at Bethel, Jacob set up the stone that he had used as a pillow and anointed it with oil. After making a vow to God, he said that if God would protect him, then the stone would be God's house. The phrase "house of God" in Hebrew is *beth-el*, from which the city of Bethel takes its name. It is clear in Genesis 28 that standing stones were accepted or at least tolerated by some practitioners of Israelite religion, but Deuteronomy regards this object as anathema to the worship of Yahweh. Similar prohibitions against standing stones are found in Exod 23:24 and Lev 26:1.

The sacred pole is better known as an Asherah pole, so named because of its connection with Asherah, a female consort of the Canaanite god Baal. These poles seem to have been made of wood, as Deut 12:3 commands that they be destroyed by burning. Deuteronomy usually links Asherah poles to standing stones, presumably because the standing stone represented the male deity while the pole was associated with the female deity. In religions in which both were worshiped together, it would be no surprise to find both objects together in the same temple. Unlike standing stones, Asherah poles, made of wood that disintegrated long ago, have not been recovered in archaeological digs. Instead, archaeologists have located holes on ritual platforms that some believe served as sockets for Asherah poles.

In forbidding these objects to be used in Israelite worship, it is unlikely that the authors of Deuteronomy were primarily concerned with the worship of other gods. A number of laws in Deuteronomy 13 prohibit such worship, but the focus in Deuteronomy 12 is different. Instead of banning the use of standing stones and Asherah poles to worship other gods, the laws in Deuteronomy 12 seem to be aimed at forbidding the use of such items to worship Yahweh. The story of

Jacob's dream at Bethel, as well as some archaeological excavations, provides evidence of the worship of Yahweh through standing stones, and Deuteronomy seems to be arguing against this practice. The concern is not which god the Israelites should worship but how to worship Yahweh. In addition, the prohibition of Asherah poles seems to be directed against those in ancient Israel who thought Yahweh had a female consort.[3]

The other issue of importance to Deuteronomy is where the Israelites were to worship God. As seen in the previous chapters, laws in Exodus, Leviticus, and Numbers allowed cultic sites to exist all over Israel. Local shrines were found in every town, and people worshiped God wherever they were. In Deuteronomy, however, multiple shrines are forbidden. Yahweh was to be worshiped in only one place, the place where God would cause his name to dwell (Deut 12:5). This was the site where all offerings had to be taken. Sacrifices couldn't be made at other locations throughout Israel but only at the central sanctuary.

Yahweh was to be worshiped in only one place, the place where God would cause his name to dwell.

Although Deuteronomy doesn't mention it specifically, it is clear that for most of the monarchic period in Israel, Jerusalem was the place where the Lord caused his name to dwell. This was to be expected, since Jerusalem was the capital of the united monarchy and the southern kingdom of Judah. Unlike some theologies in ancient Israel that saw Jerusalem as the eternal house of God, Deuteronomy viewed God's house as movable. Prior to being in Jerusalem, it had been at Mount Sinai. Later it was moved to Shiloh during the period of the judges (1 Sam 1:3 and many other passages). This is why Deuteronomy doesn't mention Jerusalem by name. Even though Jerusalem was the current dwelling place of God's name, God could decide in the future to move to another location. Jeremiah, who was influenced by the Deuteronomic tradition, used this fact in his famous Temple Sermon in Jeremiah 7. He declared that God had destroyed Shiloh because it was wicked, even though God's name had dwelled there, and God would do the same to Jerusalem if the people didn't repent (Jer 7:12–15).

But centralization of worship created a problem. According to Lev 17:1–7, any animal that was killed had to be offered as a sacrifice

81

at a tabernacle, temple, or other shrine where official priests offici-
ated. But if sacrifice could be offered only in the Jerusalem temple
during the monarchy, it would have been hard for many people to
eat meat. Jerusalem was more than a day's journey for most people,
and even those who lived in the immediate vicinity wouldn't have
wanted to go up to the temple just to prepare a meal. Deuteronomy
solves this problem by desacralizing the killing of
animals. As opposed to the system in Leviticus,
whereby any killing of an animal had to be a sacrifice, Deuteronomy divided killings into two categories. Some animals were killed for worship, and
those had to be offered as sacrifices at the temple.

Desacralizing: the opposite
of consecrating. It refers to
the act of removing the status
of holiness from an object.

Other animals could simply be slaughtered for food, and those did-
n't require the presence of a priest or an appearance at an official
sanctuary (Deut 12:15). Of course, the closing of all of the local
shrines also put the majority of priests out of business, which is why
Deuteronomy is so concerned that the Levites continued to receive
part of the tithe and be allowed to serve in Jerusalem (Deut 18:1–8).

THE KING

Unlike the legal sections in Exodus, Leviticus, and Numbers, which
make no mention of the possibility of the Israelites having a king,
Deuteronomy contains a section in 17:14–20 that not only allows for
the possibility that a king will rule in Israel but also sets up laws stating the limitations on his power. The law states that the Israelites
may have a king if they so desire but places great restraints on the
power and wealth he may accumulate. No qualifications are given
for who may serve as king, other than the requirement that he be a
native Israelite. Foreigners could not be king in Israel, a law the people seem to have followed throughout their history.

Because of the low view of kingship that Deuteronomy holds, the
limitations placed on the king were quite strict. He was not allowed
to have many horses, which amounts to a prohibition against a
standing army. He was not permitted to have numerous wives, nor is
he allowed to become wealthy. Since wealth and military power were
two of the most consistent traits of kingship in the ancient Near East,
the Deuteronomic regulations should be viewed as severely hamper-

ing the exercise of royal power in Israel. Deuteronomy requires that the king of Israel, unlike the kings of the surrounding nations, merely sit on his throne and read the law in Deuteronomy every day.

1 Samuel 8 records the setting up of Saul as the first king in Israel. In language reminiscent of Deut 17:14, the people came to Samuel, the last judge, and asked him to set a king over them to govern them "like other nations" (1 Sam 8:5). Although Samuel was upset by this request, God told him that the people were not rejecting Samuel as a leader but were rejecting Yahweh as their king (1 Sam 8:7). God then told Samuel to proceed with the appointment of a king but commanded him to tell Israel what their king would do to them:

> These will be the ways of the king who will reign over you: he will take your sons and appoint them to his chariots and to be his horsemen, and to run before his chariots; and he will appoint for himself commanders of thousands and commanders of fifties, and some to plow his ground and to reap his harvest, and to make his implements of war and the equipment of his chariots. He will take your daughters to be perfumers and cooks and bakers. He will take the best of your fields and vineyards and olive orchards and give them to his courtiers. He will take one-tenth of your grain and of your vineyards and give it to his officers and his courtiers. He will take your male and female slaves, and the best of your cattle and donkeys, and put them to his work. He will take one-tenth of your flocks, and you shall be his slaves. (1 Sam 8:11–17)

"These will be the ways of the king who will reign over you: he will take your sons and appoint them to his chariots and to be his horsemen, and to run before his chariots; and he will appoint for himself commanders of thousands and commanders of fifties." —1 Sam 8:11–12

At the very outset, the people were told that the king would break all of the laws in Deuteronomy, building up an army and amassing wealth for himself at the expense of the people. Interestingly, the king who most closely matches the description in 1 Sam 8:11–17 is Solomon. In other words, even the best of kings was viewed by Deuteronomy as problematic.

PROPHETS

In addition to being the only book in the Torah that contains laws governing kings, Deuteronomy is also unique in being the only book that contains laws about prophets. The first passage that covers prophets is found in Deut 13:1–5, which states that any prophet who encouraged the people to follow any god other than Yahweh was to be put to death. This was, in fact, the general punishment for anyone who advocated the worship of foreign gods, as shown by the verses following Deut 13:1–5. Not only prophets but even family members and entire villages could be wiped out for idolatry. One of the interesting things about the passage covering prophets, however, is that the prophet who encouraged the worship of other gods was still thought to have been sent by Yahweh. According to Deut 13:3, God used such prophets to test the people to determine if they would remain faithful to Yahweh alone.

The other passage in Deuteronomy that deals with prophets is found in 18:15–22. These verses portray prophets as continuing the function of intermediary between God and the people begun by Moses. God would send prophets to the people to speak to them, and the people were to obey such a prophet. But the office of prophet raised a number of problems for the people, chief among them being how to tell when a prophet truly was sent by God. It wasn't enough for the prophet to speak in the name of Yahweh, for anyone could make such a claim. Deuteronomy 18:22 provides an answer: any prophet whose prophecies don't come true isn't a true prophet.

While this answer may seem to solve the problem, in practice it wasn't so simple. The "solution" proposed by Deuteronomy actually created additional problems—one for the people and one for the prophet. For the people, the problem was whether to listen to a prophet when he delivered a message. If the prophet had a well-known track record of prophecies that came true, the people would know to listen to him or her. But this system wouldn't work for a new prophet. Suppose a new prophet arose with a message stating that if the people didn't do a certain action within a week, God would destroy them. Were the people to follow such a prophet? If he were a true prophet, they wouldn't have the luxury of waiting around to see if his prophecy came true, as waiting would lead to destruction. On the other hand, if they did not wait but went ahead and followed him, they could be guilty of following a false prophet, which would bring punishment as well.

The problem for the prophet is illustrated by the story of Jonah, who was told to go to Nineveh and prophesy that the city would be destroyed in forty days (Jonah 4:3). Jonah did as he was told, and the city repented. When the city repented, however, God didn't carry out the planned destruction. But this placed Jonah in an unfortunate situation. He had prophesied that the city would be destroyed in forty days, but on the forty-first day it was still standing. According to the law of Deut 18:20–22, Jonah should be seen as a false prophet, a man deserving the death penalty. This, in fact, explains Jonah's anger after the city was spared (Jonah 4:1–4). As the readers of the book of Jonah, we are also left in an uncomfortable position, since we know from the start that Jonah is a true prophet, sent by God to proclaim the imminent destruction of Nineveh. This has led some commentators to view the book of Jonah as a critique of Deuteronomy's criteria for determining true and false prophets.

HOLY WAR

Deuteronomy 20:1–20 contains laws pertaining to how the Israelites were supposed to wage war. Far from being a manual of tactics and strategy, though, this chapter presents the rules that determined who could serve in the army, as well as how the Israelites were supposed to deal with various enemies. The treatment of the spoils of war is also covered.

Having forbidden the king to keep a large standing army, Deuteronomy envisions a military drawn from the ranks of the general populace in times of need. But instead of trying to make the army as large as possible, Deuteronomy seeks to limit the army. Before a battle, the priest was to speak to the assembled troops and ask if any of them knows a reason why he shouldn't fight. Anyone who had undertaken any task—ranging from having just become engaged to having just planted a garden—but not completed it, was allowed to leave. And anyone who was afraid was asked to leave as well. Several possible explanations have been given as to why the army was kept small. One of the most popular is that it was a way of helping the people to recognize that it was God, not the people, who would win the victory (cf. Judg 7:1–7). Other explanations suggest that people who hadn't completed tasks might have been considered unholy, thereby bringing disaster on the army.

Once the composition of the army had been determined, the battle was to proceed according to who the enemy was (Deut 20:10–18).

If the opposing troops were from a city outside the land of Canaan, they were given the opportunity to surrender. Those who surrendered were made slaves. Cities that wouldn't surrender were to be attacked, and—after the inevitable victory—the men of the city were to be put to death. The women, children, and other spoils of war could be kept by the army. If the enemy lived within the boundaries of Israel, however, no offer of peace was to be made, and all men, women, children, and even livestock in those cities were to be put to death.

Deuteronomy and the Church

As the numerous references in this chapter to the books of Joshua, 1 and 2 Samuel, and 1 and 2 Kings suggest, there is a close relationship between these books and the book of Deuteronomy. Taken together, the books from Joshua to 2 Kings (without Ruth) comprise a work known as the Deuteronomistic History (DtrH). This work, composed in two or three stages at the end of the seventh and beginning of the sixth centuries, is history written from the point of view of Deuteronomy. Although written prior to the DtrH, the book of Deuteronomy itself was seen as an introduction to the DtrH, and the purpose of the DtrH was to encourage compliance with the laws in Deuteronomy. It carefully laid out the blessings and consequences of the law (cf. Deut 27–30). Kings of Israel and Judah who followed the law brought blessings upon Israel, while those who did not incurred the curses. And each king is judged on whether or not he followed the law (cf. 1 Kgs 15:1–8 and other passages). Those who obeyed are said to have done good in the sight of the Lord, while those who disobeyed are said to have done evil.

DtrH: an abbreviation for the Deuteronomistic History, a term scholars use to refer to the books of Joshua, Judges, 1 and 2 Samuel, and 1 and 2 Kings. They are called Deuteronomistic because they present the history of Israel from the point of view of the laws in Deuteronomy.

Quite aside from the theological use of Deuteronomy within the church, an understanding of Deuteronomy is necessary to facilitate the reading of the DtrH. If the content of Deuteronomy is not known, then much of the DtrH is open to misunderstanding and misinterpretation. The reign of King Manasseh of Judah (ruled 698–642 BCE) is a good illustration. By all historical standards, his kingship was a successful one. He kept the country at peace for more than fifty-five years in the face of encroaching Assyrian hegemony. He maintained good relations with Assyria while preventing his country from a rebellion that would have brought certain destruction. Yet for all this, he is given a negative rating by the DtrH (2 Kgs 21:2–9) because he violated the laws in Deut 12–13, building high places around the country and encouraging the worship of foreign gods. He is even credited with bringing about the destruction of Jerusalem and Judah through his evil acts (2 Kgs 21:10–15; 24:3), even though the kingdom was not destroyed until fifty-five years after his death. If we didn't know that Deuteronomy forbids the making of high places, the setting up of standing stones, and the erecting of Asherah poles, the condemnation of Manasseh in 2 Kings would make little sense.

Conversations with the Law in Deuteronomy

The law in Deuteronomy is a rich field for the theological imagination. The cities of refuge call us to recognize cases in which different claims for justice vie against one another and invite us to favor the side of mercy. The laws against standing stones and Asherah poles invite us to examine the innovations in our worship to see if they foster the worship of God and God alone. And the laws concerning prophets remind us of the ongoing difficulty of determining when God is speaking to us. These topics and many others are suggested by Deuteronomy. But instead of focusing on the details, as we did in previous chapters, this section will explore the role of Deuteronomy as a law intended to reform the religion of ancient Israel.

The study of the Bible throughout the history of the church has tended to emphasize the unity of the Bible instead of its diversity, with commentators explaining away discrepancies or contradictions in the text. This tendency has become even more pronounced in some Christian circles since the beginning of the Enlightenment, when rationalistic modes of reading the Bible became prominent. Theologians often have sought to determine the voice of the Bible and in doing so have reduced the variety of expressions within the text down to a single meaning. Commentators in the late nineteenth and early twentieth centuries sometimes went to the opposite extreme, however, pointing to what they considered irreconcilable differences within the Bible.

In recent years, though, scholars have begun to listen to the variety of voices within the text, letting each one speak individually without trying to enforce any kind of uniformity. This is done not to depict the Bible as a disjointed work whose authors have little in common but to highlight the variety of theological opinions, all of which may be considered orthodox even when they contradict each other or emphasize different aspects within the tradition. Such differences are clear within Deuteronomy, especially when it is read directly after a study of Exodus, Leviticus, and Numbers.

This is the approach in one of the most recent works on biblical theology, Walter Brueggemann's book *Theology of the Old Testament*, which works to establish the different voices within the Hebrew Bible.[4] The subtitle of the work, *Testimony, Dispute, and Advocacy*, makes the author's approach clear. He demonstrates that the Old Testament is not the work of a single voice but incorporates the views of majorities and minorities, the ideas of those in power and the powerless. Although his work is a difficult read for nonspecialists, it is highly rewarding for those who take the time to work through this book.

> The Old Testament isn't the work of a single voice but incorporates the views of majorities and minorities, the ideas of those in power and the powerless.

Those who seek to impose a uniformity on the text do so for a very good reason. They don't want the Bible to be seen as a random collection of texts. This is a valid goal, and one must ask whether unity is possible within a text in which a variety of voices compete to express the word of God. The answer is yes—such a unity is possible. But the unity of the Bible is not the unity of a uniform message. Instead, it is the unity of the canon. The canon, the list of books belonging to the Bible, brings with it the theological idea that all of these voices, no matter how different they are, express the word of God to the church. The canon presents us with unity without uniformity, a unity that recognizes that we don't have to agree on everything in order to be within the circle of orthodoxy. While some books definitely fall outside the bounds of orthodoxy, those that are within the canon are all Scripture, even when they don't agree.

This recognition of the diverse nature of the Scriptures has important implications for our reading of the Bible and our doing of theology. Within such a framework, each book in the Bible must be allowed to speak with its own voice so that the particular ideas of the author(s) may come through. And when we seek to use these books for constructive theology, we must not expect that everyone will reach the same conclusions or use the Bible in the same way. Since even the biblical authors did not agree, we should not expect our theology to be identical to that of other Christians, or even to that of other Anglicans. Certainly, the center of the theology will remain the same, but each will give varying emphasis to different points. That is why different books of the Bible speak to us in a variety of ways at different times, and a book that was a challenge at one point in our spiritual journey may easily become a point of comfort later on. God's word is living and active (Heb 4:12), and we should approach it in that way.

The Tapestry of the Law

The laws within the book of Deuteronomy present the reader with a program that seeks to reform the religion of ancient Israel as presented in Exodus, Leviticus, and Numbers. As a minority opinion, it seeks to change areas of life as diverse as the worship of Yahweh and the structure of the monarchy. It sets out regulations that govern everything from prophets to judicial systems to war. Presenting an alternative vision of what Israel should be, it shows us that the Bible is not a monolithic whole but a rich tapestry through which God invites people into a deeper relationship with the divine. In doing so, Deuteronomy calls us to recognize that the word of God is never the sole possession of the majority. God speaks through the minority as well.

Deuteronomy calls us to recognize that the word of God is never the sole possession of the majority.

ACKNOWLEDGMENTS

An introduction of this type always draws on information taught by so many people that it is impossible to remember what I learned from whom. I have been fortunate to have had excellent teachers throughout my academic career, and I am sure they will recognize many of their ideas reflected in these pages.

I am grateful to my professors at Carson-Newman College, most especially Donald Garner and Carolyn Blevins, who began my study of the Old Testament. Robert R. Wilson, Mark S. Smith, and Christopher Seitz at Yale continued to feed my fascination with the Bible, as did P. Kyle McCarter Jr. at the Johns Hopkins University. A special note of thanks goes to Raymond Westbrook at Hopkins, a former lawyer and now specialist in biblical law.

It has been a pleasure to work with the people at Morehouse. Debra Farrington and Nancy Fitzgerald have worked as editors on this series, and Ryan Masteller has seen this work through to the final stages. My location in Eastern Europe has made it more difficult for them, but their patience and creative solutions have made the process run very smoothly. My gratitude also goes to Frederick Schmidt, our general editor. Fred conceived this series as a way for the Anglican Association of Biblical Scholars to serve the church, and I can only hope that this volume will help achieve that goal.

I am also grateful to a number of people who have helped in various ways. Bess Garrett provided housing in Baltimore when I was home from Lithuania and needed to do research at the Johns Hopkins library. Kathleen W. Bowman and Tony Bowman both read drafts of several chapters, and their comments helped strengthen the manuscript. And students in my Pentateuch classes at Lithuania Christian College have helped me tailor the text for an audience interested in how the legal sections of the Torah can be used as Scripture in the church.

As always, my greatest thanks go to my family. My wife Stephanie has assisted in many ways, from personal encouragement to reading drafts. As a priest, she is constantly challenging me to answer the "so what?" questions, i.e., "What practical difference can the study of this material make in the lives of those who read it?" If this book teaches you ways to incorporate the Pentateuch into your life as a Christian, you have her to thank for that. My children, Duncan and Emma, are always there to remind me there is more to life than academics. They have been willing to let me write when it was time to write, but insistent that I stop when it was time to play. They have a remarkable knack for telling the difference between the two.

STUDY QUESTIONS
The Reverend Helen McPeak

Grounded in his lifelong respect for and wrestling with the Bible, Kevin A. Wilson brings both professorial and parenting experience into play as he seeks to bring the Law more naturally into conversations with the daily life of faith. With a strong critical mind and clear commitment to continuing the dialogue, he offers straightforward information about the biblical laws which calls us to reclaim and seek wisdom in this part of our scriptural canon.

Introduction

Before you begin, think about how you experience laws in your life (e.g. laws of physics, traffic laws, family rules, religious laws, school rules, civil laws, etc.). What roles do laws play?

Pray together for God's guidance and support in this study you are beginning.
- What are your hopes for this learning?
- Why do you engage it now?
- How will you open yourself to receive what God will give?

What is your understanding of the Law in Scripture?
- How were you introduced to the Law?
- What role does it play in your life at this time?

Where is the Law a blessing? Where a curse?

What is your working definition of the Law?
- Is it an "official set of rules"? Is it "instruction"?
- List the eight synonyms Psalm 119 uses to convey the idea of *torah*.

Do you agree with Wilson's assertion that "Except for the Ten Commandments, Christians don't pay much attention to the Laws of the Pentateuch" (p. xvii)? Why or why not?

What has been passed to you orally from parents, teachers, grandparents, friends, neighbors, ministers, etc.? What came through nonverbally?

The people of Israel found definition of their identity in the narratives and legal texts of the Pentateuch. What sources define your identity corporately? Individually?

What familiarity do you have with the sources J, E, D, and P and research on Documentary Hypothesis? If this is one, what other hypotheses exist?

Wilson explains the rhythm he will use to lead us through this study: a look at the text, presentation of some background information, then rationale behind the laws and the way they functioned in the life of ancient Israel. He invites us to come with expectation for some contemporary application. What in your experience with scripture supports this expectation? What hinders it?

Chapter One: The Ten Commandments

Quick, before you look: Can you name all ten of the commandments? (No peeking!) Write them down.

What were you taught about the Ten Commandments as a child? How were you taught? Has this approach changed over time?

Revisit Wilson's comparison of Exodus 20:1–17 and Deuteronomy 5:6–21. What do you observe about the delivery? The date?

Wilson writes that "in the centuries prior to [the completion of Exodus], the contents of the Ten Commandments may have been in flux" (p. 3).
- How does this affect your view of the biblical story of the Ten Commandments?
- Is it difficult for you to let go of your image of God's hand handing down the stone tablets as the first delivery of these ideas?

Read Exodus 34:17–26, Leviticus 19:1–19, and Deuteronomy 27:15–26. What themes and generalities do you see in these Decalogue-like formations?

Wilson writes, "the Ten Commandments deal primarily with the overarching ideas concerning how the people are to relate to God and to others" (p. 5). He further suggests some reasons why the Ten Commandments were selected to serve as the center of Israelite law. Revisit this discussion.
- To what is the Decalogue not tied?
- Why is this relevant?
- What focus arose from this freedom?

Wilson writes that the Ten Commandments are not so named in Exodus 20 or Deuteronomy 5 (p. 5–6).
- How might you title this set of laws?
- What difference does it make?

Discuss the difference in emphases Wilson highlights between Anglicans (and many others in the Reformed tradition) and Roman Catholics and Lutherans (p. 6). Why do you suppose this difference abides?

Wilson writes that "interpersonal relationships must be seen in the light of our relation to the divine" (p. 6). Give some examples of this illumination in your own life, your community.

Wilson explores the statement that God is "a jealous God punishing children for the iniquity of parents, to the third and fourth generation of those who reject me" (Exodus 20:5).
- With which of the explanations offered do you more closely resonate?
- What other interpretations come to mind?

Reexamine the two rationales for the Sabbath from Deuteronomy and Exodus highlighted by Wilson (p. 10).
- Explore the interplay between the two.
- Which motivates you?
- How do you follow the commandment to keep the Sabbath holy?

Which Commandment most engages your attention at this time?
- With what do you struggle?
- How has your relationship the Law evolved over time?

Revisit Wilson's discussion of the final six commandments (p. 11–15).
- How might these apply in life today?
- Where do we expand the Commandments?
- Where do we limit the original intention (e.g. capital punishment, unfaithful spouses, inheritance, retention of property, honesty, inner disposition, etc.)?

So what?
- How does your deepened intellectual understanding of these basic requirements of the life of faith call you to action?
- What will you do differently because you are engaging in this study?

Chapter Two: The Law in Exodus

Review the four sections of the Law as defined by Fretheim that Wilson cites. In what ways does this division "keep the law firmly rooted in the life of the people" (p. 20)?

Wilson states, "Woven into the cloth of [the Exodus story], the law isn't divine directive imposed on the people from outside, but part of the same plan as the deliverance from Egypt and the covenant at Sinai: God has called a people for his own" (p. 20).

- How does the law interweave with the salvation of Israel from Egypt?
- How does the law interweave with the whole salvation history?

Revisit Wilson's discussions of the origins of the Covenant Code content (p. 20).

- Who is most likely responsible for this code?
- When does it become a part of the people's history?
- How important are these details of origin to your relationship with the code?

Wilson calls our attention to the division of the Book of the Covenant (Exodus 21:1–23:19) into two sections: *casuistic* and *apodictic*.

- Where else do you find these words defined? Explore their definitions.
- Play with them. Write your own examples of each type. Make up a chant to help you remember.
- Which type do you prefer?

Read the Covenant Code (Exodus 20:22–23:33). Wilson suggests that "the fact that these two laws are included within the covenant-making process itself points to the importance that they had in ancient Israel as well as the centrality biblical authors ascribe to them" (p. 22).

- What is your initial reaction to these laws?
- Why do you suppose this "collection of rules" is given such importance?

In the midst of some arbitrary and obscure laws (e.g. 21:7 and 23:5) lie some laws which have become central to contemporary understanding of God's expectations (e.g. *lex talionis*: 21:23–25 and 22:21–27).

- How do you discern the most appropriate application of particular laws in your own life?

How do you respond to Wilson's comments that "the text goes into great—almost excruciating—detail, and these are not the most exciting chapters in the book of Exodus" (p. 26)?

- How much time do you give to this "topic to which the Scriptures give so much space"? Why?

Go ahead! Watch *Raiders of the Lost Ark*.

- Look at the model of the ark as Wilson suggests.
- Sketch it.
- Model it with Play-Doh.
- What do you notice?

Try to make sense of the text in Exodus 26–27.

- Sketch the layout of the tabernacle and accoutrements as described in the Bible.
- Where would you be allowed to stand?
- How might it feel to worship in his space?

Wilson asks, "How can we use the laws in Exodus for life within the Church today?" Good question!

- Review Wilson's explanation of the historical and theological difficulties (p. 28–29).
- What suggestions does he offer for claiming the value of these Scriptures?
- What patterns of life are put forth by the law?

Wilson states, "Within the faith community, everything is within God's purview" (p. 32).

- Into what areas of your life do you invite God?
- Which areas do you prefer to handle alone?

- Where is God most visible in your community?
- Where is God most needed?

What in your life has been akin to building the tabernacle, both in terms of demanding detailed attention and in terms of supporting your nearness to God?

Chapter Three: Sacrifices in Leviticus

In the broadest sense of the word, what sacrifices have you made in your life?
- What motivated your sacrifice?
- How do you feel when making an offering to God?

Read Leviticus 1–7.
- Name the offerings listed in v. 7:37.

Wilson offers a list of things to note in studying these offerings (p. 34).
- Review this list

Wilson writes, "Animals with some kind of defect were not acceptable offerings, for a perfect God requires perfect sacrifices" (p. 35; see also the need for temple holiness on p. 38). How has this idea evolved to the point where we now offer to God a "sacrifice of praise and thanksgiving" (Eucharistic Prayer C, Book of Common Prayer, p. 371)?

What explanations have you encountered for the placing of the offerand's hands on the animal to be sacrificed?
- Why is this important?
- What assumptions are made about offerings in your own worship?

Wilson distinguishes the Israelite idea of sacrifice from those of the cultures around them (p. 36). What point is made in this distinction?

Wilson reminds us, "So any time the people wanted to eat meat, they had to offer a sacrifice" (p. 38).

- Compare this with your own experience of meat in your diet today.
- What facet of health is emphasized in each model?

Having read these laws regarding specific parts of animals, what will you do?

- Will you continue to eat liver and kidney pie?
- Will you enjoy paté and gravy?
- Why? How will you decide?

Wilson discussed the concept that God "cannot dwell in an impure place" (p. 38).

- What would happen when the temple became unfit for God's presence?
- How powerful would this motivation be in your own religious practice?

Compare and contrast methods of confession and absolution today with methods of acknowledgment of unintentional sin and purification described in this chapter.

- What beliefs are reflected?
- What roles are elucidated?

Wilson writes, "We often think of the Old Testament sacrificial system as an arrangement that worked fine until Jesus came, but became unnecessary once he arrived . . . (though this) doesn't do justice to the purpose and place of offerings in the life of ancient Israel" (p. 42).

- Revisit his description of why the majority of sacrifices were offered.
- Why is ritual important?
- What parallels do you find between the worship of the ancient Israelites and our own? (Wilson names 3.)

Wilson asserts, "The perils of corporate sins outweigh those of individual misdeeds" (p. 44–45).

- What examples of corporate sin today can you name?
- What one step are you willing to take toward returning the community to right relationship with God?

Explore the tensions between the ideas of Leviticus 1–7 as Wilson develops them and such passages as Mark 2:17. What purity is required of us in today's understanding in our interaction with God?

Chapter Four: The Law in Leviticus

Jot down in your own words a definition of "holiness."

Revisit the two extremes Wilson names between which we are to use the Law in a theologically helpful way (pp. 49–50). Toward which do you more often lean?

Wilson calls our attention to the 39 Articles of Religion established in the United States in 1801 (BCP, p. 867ff). These 200-year-old American Articles may feel as distant as their 435-year-old originals or as the 2,500-year-old laws of ancient Israel.

- What wisdom do you glean from perusing them?
- What role does external authority play in your faith life?

Studying law in community can be an act of faith.

- What reactions do you have to such laws Wilson highlights as the law about which water creatures may be eaten; or the simple existence of, as well as the different durations of, ritual uncleanness of a woman following childbirth of a male or female child; or the laws governing mildew?
- What impact do these laws have on your life?

Stepping back from the individual points of the Holiness Code allows us to regain focus on its unifying theme of holiness: "You shall be holy, for I the Lord your God am holy" (Leviticus 19:2).

- How do the individual points support or distract from this theme?
- What reasons does Wilson give for its importance?

Wilson offers new ways of looking at Leviticus (pp. 56–59). Revisit these.

Explore his definition of holiness (p. 56).

- How does it compare with what you wrote down as you began to study this chapter?
- What patterns of living emerge from Leviticus to bring you into closer relationship with God?

Wilson, an expert on the Old Testament, writes, "Only as a whole is the Bible a sufficient witness to God's actions, and when we don't treat it as a whole we skew our perspective of God (p. 58).

- How do these particular specialized insights draw you more deeply into the presence of God in your daily faith journey?
- For what does this knowledge better equip you?

As Wilson explores the continuity of covenants, what similarities and differences does he articulate (p. 58)? What helps you to truly comprehend the reality of God's action in lives both in ancient times and in the here and now?

Wilson writes, "It's far too easy to become so at home with the Bible that it never challenges us" (p. 59).

- In your experience, is this danger real? Why?
- How is this study supporting the Bible's challenge to you?

Chapter Five: The Law in Numbers

What are the largest groups of laws Wilson delineates for us in Numbers? How are they distributed?

Wilson writes, "Although the tabernacle at the center of the encampment symbolized God's place at the center of their communal life, the holiness of the tabernacle was a danger to the people" (p. 65).

- What in modern life can you think of that is also central and dangerous?
- Who are the "priests" of these things?

In what ways did the Levites serve as a substitution (p. 66)?

- What did God accept from them?
- In place of what?
- Who serves that function today?

What assumptions underlie the laws concerning women in Numbers?

- How do you respond to the point Wilson makes that "unlike in some societies, the woman is not automatically considered guilty" (p. 66)?
- Upon what does the value lie in the examples of the daughters of Zelophehad?

In discussing *nazarites*, Wilson comments, "the precise purpose of each rule isn't always clear" and "the purpose for taking such a vow isn't (clear)."

- What explanations can you imagine for these laws?
- What role have vows, lifelong or temporary, played in your own life?

Revisit Wilson's exploration of the applications Levitical laws have within the Church today (pp. 70–72).

- How might study of the law undergird the sense of holiness and reverence with which such service is performed?
- What are the possibilities for nazarite-type service available today?
- How could an entire congregation be involved?

In what ministries are you currently engaged which serve the world, the altar, or both? How does this study encourage and challenge you?

Chapter Six: The Law in Deuteronomy

What difference does Wilson cite as one enters the book of Deuteronomy after Exodus, Leviticus, and Numbers? Familiarize yourself with Source Theory, Documentary Hypothesis, using exegetical resources.

In what way is Deuteronomy a misnomer?
- When in history does this book of law make an appearance?
- What effects does the discovery of this book have?
- What similarities does Wilson highlight between the laws in Deuteronomy and those in Exodus through Numbers?

Revisit the Decalogue as you read Wilson's exploration of Braulik's and Wright's work corresponding the Decalogue and the law in Deuteronomy. What do you notice?

How is justice served by the cities of refuge described in Numbers 35 and Deuteronomy 19? What purpose do they serve? (For an interesting sidebar, compare and contrast this concept with that of the Cities of Asylum Network in our contemporary society.)

Wilson describes particular traits and foci of Deuteronomic laws governing worship. Revisit these laws (pp. 79–82).
- What important facets of worship are addressed?
- What are some key facets of your own worship today?

In exploring the Deuteronomic laws affecting the king, Wilson asserts that God interprets to Samuel the people's actions (p. 83).
- Review this interpretation.
- What are the results of the people's choice?

What criterion does Deuteronomy put forth for determining a true prophet (Deuteronomy 18:22)?
- What double bind might this bring?
- What criteria assist you in discerning the authenticity of prophets today?

What guidelines regarding the making of war does Wilson elucidate in Deuteronomy? (How) might these laws be useful guidance today?

Wilson writes that "the Law in Deuteronomy is a rich field for the theological imagination (p. 87). He lists several examples.
- In what ways does the law in Deuteronomy stir your imagination?
- How is it for you to allow "the variety of voices within the text . . . each [to] speak individually without trying to enforce any kind of uniformity" (p. 88)?
- How much internal contradiction or variations of emphases can orthodoxy tolerate?
- How do you respond to "unity without uniformity" (p. 88)?

What "take-home message" do you find in this "rich tapestry through which God invites people to deeper relationship with the divine" (p. 89)?

The Rev. Helen McPeak serves as Priest Associate at the Episcopal Church of the Epiphany in Henderson, Nevada. Her current manifestation as wife and mother in Las Vegas is lived largely in accordance with the laws of the Pentateuch.

NOTES

Introduction to the Series

1. David F. Ford, "The Bible, the World and the Church I," in *The Official Report of the Lambeth Conference 1998* (ed. J. Mark Dyer et al.; Harrisburg, Pa.: Morehouse Publishing, 1999), 332.
2. For my broader understanding of authority, I am indebted to Eugene Kennedy and Sara C. Charles, *Authority: The Most Misunderstood Idea in America* (New York: Free Press, 1997).
3. William Sloane Coffin, *Credo* (Louisville: Westminster John Knox Press, 2003), 156.

Chapter One: The Ten Commandments

1. See chapter 4.
2. A. D. H. Mayes, *Deuteronomy*, New Century Bible Commentary (Grand Rapids: Eerdmans, 1981), 167.
3. Terence Fretheim, *Exodus*, Interpretation (Louisville, Ky.: John Knox Press, 1991), 231.
4. Jacob Milgrom, *Leviticus*, Anchor Bible 3A (New York: Doubleday, 2000), 1637.

Chapter Two: The Law in Exodus

1. Terence Fretheim, *Exodus*, 201–7.
2. For convenience, all references are taken from laws that are found in Bill T. Arnold and Bryan E. Beyer, *Readings from the Ancient Near East*, Encountering Biblical Studies (Grand Rapids: Baker, 2002). Cited as *RANE*.

Chapter Three: Sacrifices in Leviticus

1. A better term for these gifts would be *offerings*, as not all of the gifts are animals. It is hardly appropriate to refer to a grain sacrifice, since grain cannot be killed. Nevertheless, because the term *sacrifice* is so closely related to all these offerings, the traditional terminology will be used here.

2. The meaning of the laying on of hands is often taken to signify the transference of guilt from the offerand to the animal. Milgrom has pointed out, however, that such a transference in the scapegoat ritual (Lev 16:21) requires both hands, and therefore such a meaning is not present in the burnt offering. Jacob Milgrom, *Leviticus: A Book of Ritual and Ethics* (Minneapolis: Fortress Press, 2004), 24. The fact that the laying on of hands occurs again in the instructions for the sacrifice of well-being (Lev 3:2), an offering that does not remove sin, reinforces this interpretation.
3. The fat indicated here is only the suet that is found around the entrails. Obviously, the fat that is part of the meat cannot be separated.
4. Jacob Milgrom, *Leviticus 1–16*, Anchor Bible 3 (New York: Doubleday, 1998), 301–2.
5. Allen P. Ross, *Holiness to the Lord: A Guide to the Exposition of the Book of Leviticus* (Grand Rapids: Baker, 2002).
6. Samuel E. Balentine, "Review of *Holiness to the Lord: A Guide to the Exposition of the Book of Leviticus,*" *Catholic Biblical Quarterly* 65.3 (2003): 453–54.

Chapter Four: The Law in Leviticus

1. Gordan D. Fee and Douglas Stuart, *How to Read the Bible for All Its Worth*, 3rd ed. (Grand Rapids: Zondervan, 2003).
2. Fee and Stuart, *How to Read the Bible*, 167 (italics in original).
3. The Book of Common Prayer according to the Use of the Episcopal Church of the USA (New York: Church Hymnal Corporation, 1979), 869.
4. The metaphor is taken from Jacob's wrestling with God at the river Jabbok in Gen 32:22–32. While in the context of Genesis it refers to striving with God, the image is also a helpful one in approaching the Scriptures.

Chapter Five: The Law in Numbers

1. It is worth noting that the focus on shaving Samson's head parallels the emphasis that the book of Numbers places on the consecrated head of the Nazirite.

Chapter Six: The Law in Deuteronomy

1. G. Braulik, "The Sequence of the Laws in Deuteronomy 12–26 and in the Decalogue," *A Song of Power and the Power of Song*, ed. D. L. Christensen (Winona Lake, Ind.: Eisenbrauns, 1993), 313–35. For a commentary that follows this scheme in its treatment of the laws, see Mark E. Biddle, *Deuteronomy*, Smyth & Helwys Bible Commentary (Macon, Ga.: Smyth & Helwys, 2003).

2. The chart follows the discussion of the arrangement of Deut 12–26 in Christopher Wright, *Deuteronomy*, New International Bible Commentary, ed. Robert L. Hubbard Jr. and Robert K. Johnson (Peabody, Mass.: Hendrickson, 1996), 4–5.
3. Inscriptions discovered at Kuntillet ʿAjrud on the Sinai Peninsula as well as a temple at Arad with two standing stones suggest that some in Israel thought that Yahweh had a female counterpart.
4. Walter Brueggemann, *Theology of the Old Testament: Testimony, Dispute, and Advocacy* (Minneapolis: Augsburg Fortress Press, 1997).

SUGGESTIONS
FOR FURTHER READING

The explorations of the law in this book are, of necessity, only a beginning. The overview that this book offers can only begin to suggest the theological and spiritual riches that await those who explore further. The books listed here are intended to aid in that search. Each section provides a recommendation of commentaries that are scholarly yet accessible to non-specialists. Several monographs that will help the reader focus on individual issues are also included.

Ten Commandments

A number of books have come out on the subject of the Ten Commandments in recent years. For another treatment from an Anglican perspective, see G. Corwin Stoppel, *Living Words: The Ten Commandments in the Twenty-First Century* (Cambridge, Mass.: Cowley, 2005). Also good is Stanley M. Hauerwas and William H. Willimon, *The Truth About God: The Ten Commandments in Christian Life* (Nashville: Abingdon, 1999). For a look at how the Decalogue has been approached by various thinkers throughout history, see Paul Grimley Kuntz, *The Ten Commandments in History: Mosaic Paradigms for a Well-Ordered Society* (Grand Rapids: Eerdmans, 2004).

Exodus

Brevard Childs, *The Book of Exodus*, WOTL (Philadelphia: Westminster, 1974) is an excellent commentary. Childs approaches the text from a theological perspective that directly addresses the question of how Exodus functions as Christian scripture. Childs is well versed in the history of Jewish and Christian interpretation of Exodus, which introduces readers to what is often an unexplored area of biblical studies. Another worthwhile commentary is Terence E. Fretheim, *Exodus*, Interpretation (Louisville: Westminster/John Knox, 1991). Fretheim does a good job covering the Decalogue and the Covenant Code, although his treatment of the tabernacle material is a little short.

Leviticus

By far the best commentary on Leviticus is Jacob Milgrom, *Leviticus*, 3 vols., Anchor Bible 3 (New York: Doubleday, 1991, 2000, 2001). The three volumes total an impressive 2,713 pages, containing far more information than the average reader would ever need. But for those who want help on the interpretation of a particular verse, this is the place to go. If you are looking for a more accessible volume, Milgrom's one-volume commentary from Fortress Press is much more readable (Jacob Milgrom, *Leviticus: A Book of Ritual and Ethics*, Continental Commentaries [Minneapolis: Fortress Press, 2004]). Milgrom approaches the text from a Jewish background, which brings a dimension to his commentary that may be unfamiliar yet welcome to Christian readers. From the Christian side, Samuel Balentine, *Leviticus*, Interpretation (Louisville: Westminster/John Knox, 2002) is a very good commentary that explores the theological issues with an eye toward the church.

One of the few recent books to explore how Leviticus can be used in the church is Allen P. Ross, *Holiness to the Lord: A Guide to the Exposition of the Book of Leviticus* (Grand Rapids: Baker, 2002). Although the book has shortcomings (see chapter 3), it is still noteworthy for its effort to read Leviticus as Christian Scripture. Ross approaches the book from a more evangelical perspective than most Anglicans, but those who work through his book will come away with a sense of the issues and the importance of engaging Leviticus in the church. Another way to delve deeper into Leviticus can be found in Lester L. Grabbe, *Leviticus*, Old Testament Guides, ed. R. N. Whybray (Sheffield: Sheffield Academic Press, 1993). If the reader's interest is in the worship of Israel in general, a succinct guide can be found in Walter Brueggeman, *Worship in Israel: An Essential Guide* (Nashville: Abingdon, 2005).

Numbers

Those looking for an in-depth commentary on Numbers will be well served by Baruch A. Levine, *Numbers*, 2 vols., Anchor Bible 4 (New York: Doubleday, 1993, 2000). The Interpretation commentary series is usually a good place to find a Christian approach to the text, and Denis T. Olson, *Numbers*, Interpretation (Louisville: Westminster/John Knox, 1996) is no exception. Although one might wish for a more in-depth coverage in places, it will certainly help the reader come to a better understanding of the text. Timothy R. Ashley, *The Book of Numbers*, New International Commentary on the Old Testament (Grand Rapids: Eerdmans, 1993) structures its reading of Numbers around the theme of obedience and disobedience to God.

Deuteronomy

Mark E. Biddle, *Deuteronomy*, Smyth & Helwys Bible Commentary (Macon, Ga.: Smyth & Helwys, 2003) is a good next step for those wanting to delve deeper into Deuteronomy. Biddle not only examines the meaning of the text, but a "Connections" section after each chapter explores ways that the text can be appropriated within the church. Sidebars and an accompanying CD-ROM make this commentary quite accessible. Patrick D. Miller, *Deuteronomy*, Interpretation (Louisville: Westminster/John Knox, 1990) is also a good commentary, although the law in Deuteronomy 12–26 receives only seventy pages of treatment. Peter C. Craige, *The Book of Deuteronomy*, New International Commentary on the Old Testament (Grand Rapids: Eerdmans, 1976) is worthwhile as well.

ABOUT THE AUTHOR

Kevin A. Wilson received a B.A. in religion and political science from Carson-Newman College. He did his seminary at Yale Divinity School, where he earned both an M.Div. and an S.T.M. He completed his graduate work at the Johns Hopkins University with a Ph.D. in Old Testament. He has taught Old Testament as an adjunct at Virginia Theological Seminary (Alexandria, VA) and biblical studies as a lecturer at Wartburg College (Waverly, IA).

Kevin currently teaches biblical studies at Lithuania Christian College in Klaipeda, Lithuania, a post he has held since 2004. Lithuania Christian College was founded in 1991 as the Soviet Union collapsed and Lithuania regained its independence. Because it is a relatively new college, it relies on faculty who raise their own support. Kevin and his wife, the Rev. Stephanie Chase Wilson, serve in Klaipeda as appointed missionaries of the Episcopal Church. Stephanie is the pastor of the local English speaking congregation. They have two children, Duncan and Emma.

Kevin regularly leads Bible studies in the parishes where his wife serves as rector, most recently in the Church of the Redeemer (Baltimore, MD) and All Saints' Episcopal Church (Sunderland, MD). He is frequently a guest speaker in parishes in the Episcopal Dioceses of Maryland and Washington, DC. He also serves on the executive board of the Anglican Association of Biblical Scholars.